YOU CAN'T STEAL
FIRST BASE

YOU
CAN'T
STEAL
FIRST
BASE

Charles Granville Hamilton

PHILOSOPHICAL LIBRARY
New York

Appreciation is given for the republication of sermons which have appeared in the *Aberdeen Examiner, African Methodist Episcopal Church Review, Amory Advertiser, Anglican Outlook, Baptist Student, Baptist Training Union Quarterly, Centennial Sermons, Christian, Christian Century, Christian Outlook, Churchman, Crossroads, Forward, Jackson Clarion Ledger, Living Church, Memphis Press Scimitar, Mississippi Methodist Advocate, Muncie Star, Nashville Tennessean, Presbyterian Journal* and other publications.

Copyright, 1971, by PHILOSOPHICAL LIBRARY, INC.,
15 East 40th Street, New York, N. Y. 10016

Library of Congress Catalog Card No. 74-164909
SBN 8022-2057-6

PRINTED IN THE UNITED STATES OF AMERICA

To

MARY ELIZABETH

WHO HAS SHARED THIS MINISTRY
WITH FAITH, HOPE AND LOVE

Contents

YOU CAN'T STEAL FIRST BASE

Did you ever try playing baseball with children too young to understand a game has to have rules and who wanted to take five strikes or to steal first base? You had to explain that you can't steal first base. You can steal your way to other bases, but not to first. You may get to first base by a hit or an error or a base on balls, but you can't steal first base. This is the rule, and you can not have a game without rules.

The game of life has many resemblances to the game of baseball. You can't steal first base in the great game of living. You have to learn the rules of the game of life. Many of the rules are negative. In this age of yes-men it is hard to say "No." The third word the Apostle Paul used in Galatians was "Not." When Gresham Machen spent a whole period on this word in our Princeton class, we wondered how we would ever get through the book at that rate. But he did convince us of the importance of the negative. The spirit which says "No" has always been associated with the divine. Socrates declared that the divine guidance which came to him was always negative. Aristotle noted that 9 of 10 ideas and impulses which came to us are to be answered "No." To be always positive and never negative is the mark of a false prophet. Remember Micaiah, outnumbered 400-1 for his negative truth against positive lies? In Grindal, Norway, stands a monument to 17,000 who suffered at the Nazi concentration camp, on it the one word "No."

The two brave "Noes" of the bishops of Cajazzo and Little Rock at the 1870 Vatican Council were the hope for the future. Every negative involves a positive. Fences are negative devices for positive results in keeping some in and some out. Stoplights are negative half the time, but they achieve positive results in saving life at the inevitable intersections of existence. You have to tear down an old shack if you want to replace it with a better

1

building. You arrive at a positive conclusion by negative means when you discover something you have been taught as history is not true. Biblical pictures of heaven are negatives from which are developed the hope of no night, no pain, no sin, no death, no tears.

The negative which Galatians emphasizes is that the Christian faith is not human religion. The apostle insists that he is a missionary sent from God with a message from God, not sent from man. He makes no appeal on the basis of his own personality as an intellectual Roman Jew or on his record of writing, preaching, working, suffering. The faith he proclaims is not to be adjusted to the inadequate insights of any age; it cannot accommodate itself to the transient fashions of thought and action of any era.

The apostle is careful to point out that he is not an apostle of man or through man. He claims no apostolic succession. He is careful to repudiate any connection with the other apostles. None of them called him or ordained him. He is not the salesman for an ecclesiastical chain store. It is no human religion he presents and represents. No church sent him, no bishop laid hands on him, no presbytery sent him forth, no congregation called him. His call came directly from God, his divine commission from Christ. The only apostolic succession is walking in the ways of the apostles, which is far from the false apostles of the past and present who have a succession from Judas. To claim succession from past prelates of insolence is as useless as a buggywhip on a streamlined automobile. You do not keep your grandfather's tradition of being the best dressed man in town by wearing his ragged overcoat.

This is the present evil world, as the apostle noted. It is evil, it has been evil, it will be evil. It killed the best Man who ever lived, and it tries to kill all who follow in His way. The world glorifies and promotes the thieves, murderers and liars who run it. This evil world is always inescapably present. Christ began a permanent revolution against the evil world and His followers are permanent revolutionists against the works of the devil which constitute this world order.

Human religion is the counterfeit this present evil world tries

2

to sell you, the vaccination to make you immune to the genuine faith of Jesus. The apostle began his other epistles with kind words of praise, but the error in this church is too serious for such. While he dictated his other epistles to secretaries because of his own weak eyes, he scrawls out this epistle in large letters because of its urgency. False apostles have come in to try to substitute a counterfeit religion of outward ceremony for inward faith. The curse of the Eternal is upon all such counterfeit religion.

Those who seemed important held no awe for him, but he shared the common faith of the other apostles in caring for the poor. This is the litmus paper to test faith; any faith that helps the poor is of Jesus, and faith that is not concerned for the poor is not of Jesus, no matter how often it mouths His name. The apostles agree; the faith which gives a hungry man only words will not save.

UNLESS YOU BELONG TO THE TEAM

You can't play unless you belong to the team. There is no place in the game for someone who wants to play, but who refuses to join either team. It is the team which wins, not the individuals. You can't do much in life unless you play on the team. The apostle was the star pitcher of the team, but he added the brothers as authors of the letters, because he was part of the team.

You can not improve an organization from the outside. If you can do good in an organization, you need to belong to it. You can not influence government by staying outside the parties through which it is run. You do not leave the party because you do not like the pitcher for the day. We can not operate apart from other states or other nations. You make the church no better by not belonging, not attending, not teaching, not singing, not giving. If you love God, you will want to worship more than once a week. The only way to improve government,

3

education, church is to go into them with a purpose to better them.

"You can not see my face unless your brother be with you," as Joseph told his brothers, is what God tells us. Conversion is only the front end of faith; solitary faith is imaginary; you can not love God and not love your neighbor. Jesus says to leave your gift and not bring it to the altar until you have made peace with your brother, even if this wrecks the every member canvass.

God does not suggest you love your neighbor, He commands it. He does not require you to like your neighbor but to want him to live as well as you do. If you love your neighbor, you will not sell him anything at a price you would not want to pay, you will not do less work than you would want done by someone working for you, you will not pay him less than you think you ought to be paid; you will not rent him a house in which you would not want to live.

To earn a living is a Christian duty, but to keep more than you need is not loving your neighbor. This is why Jesus made it clear that a rich man can not see heaven. Those with more dollars than sense do not love their neighbors; if they did, they would give away their riches. Give all you can. Because of the meanness of the rich, taxation is better than charitable organizations because it takes from those who have more than they need and gives to those who have less. Anyone who is against giving welfare to those genuinely in need makes himself an enemy of God. You vote yourself out of heaven if you vote for a candidate who promises to do less for the poor. "We know we have crossed the frontier from death to life because we love the brothers," as Phillipps translates.

No one enjoys watching grandstand players. "If I were still pleasing men, I would not be the servant of God," reminds the apostle. "If it be preached in peace, it is not the gospel," noted Luther. You can either please your children or love them. If you let your boy have seven chocolate ice cream cones, you have harmed him for your own selfish ease. A teacher who gives correct grades is not popular but in the long run is respected while those who tried to please are scorned. A doctor can please his

4

patients or can help them. A politician may look to the next election and play on the ignorance of his constituents, but a statesman looks to the next generation and serves them. A minister may cater to the prejudices of members, fail to warn them of the results of their sins, adopt their moods and adapt the gospel to their low levels of life, but they will not call for him when in need; they will prefer one who told the truth when it was unpopular. Woodrow Wilson noted that the American Revolution was to change the world, not to please it.

Do not measure interest in faith only by those who attend church. Only 1,000,000 people a day attend major league baseball games, but millions more read of them, listen to them, see them on a screen. More go to church than to ball games, clubs, movies or the polls. More believe in decency than you may think. There are more homes of love than of headlines. More worship Christ than any other.

The little boy who wondered, "Daddy, why does the church have a plus sign on it?" was correct. Its wood and bricks witness to more than other buildings. Worship is a plus sign which adds deeps and heights to our days. Uniting our voices in hymns of hope adds strength. Prayer is a plus to God's daily donations. The Word is a plus to other words and the sermon a plus to understanding. The cross is a plus sign of what God gave and of what God asks. Faith does not change the furniture in the room of life, but it turns on the light that we may see and know. Eternal life fulfills what is finest and adds new horizons and scarlet dawns of radiant and unending tomorrows.

Some years ago a black minister was waiting for a train in a small town in Mississippi, and he said that because he came from Georgia he was afraid to go in the white waiting room, although it was raining and the other waiting room was closed for repairs. The white agent urged him to come out of the rain into the warmth and fire of the white waiting room. Finally the agent pulled him into the room. As the train came the minister lingered to thank his benefactor, but the agent refused to accept any thanks. "I didn't do it for you"; he insisted, "it ain't good for me for you to be outside."

YOU CAN'T EARN A BASE ON BALLS

You cannot earn a base on balls. It is given to you. The pitcher throws four high or wide, and you get to first base without doing a thing. But you did not earn it. You cannot tell the pitcher: "Look, I'm so good you have to give me a base on balls." For you aren't; and he doesn't have to give it. It is free.

Life is full of what is given. Most of us were given American citizenship at birth; we did not earn it. The opportunity for an education is given to us. Our families were given to us; we were not entitled to the home in which we grew up. Great thoughts come to our minds. Scientists testify that when they reached a point where their reason could go no further, the idea came to them. Inventors testify that the last link in their chain of construction came to them. A poet cannot sit down and decide to write a poem; poetry comes to him. Life is largely a matter of the given.

The grace of God is, reverently speaking, a base on balls. We do not earn it or merit it. We do not deserve it. We cannot buy it. It is given to us, freely, regardless of our own deserving. Nothing you do can put God in debt to you. There is no way to earn merit with God by creed or cult, person or place. It all comes of His free overwhelming grace and love for you and me.

The grace of God is also like a base on balls in that you do not have to take it. You do not have to take a base on balls. Even if the balls are out of reach, you can strike at them and fan out. You do not have to take the gifts of God. You do not have to take the sunlight; you can shut yourself in the dark. You do not have to take the gift of air, though I am not suggesting you stop breathing. You can go through the cafeteria line of education and take nothing.

Abraham was accepted by God through faith before he began an outward religion. Faith precedes its outward expression. Neither religion nor irreligion will save you, but faith working

6

in love. The church must have something divine in it to have survived the ministers and members it has had. Paul was distressed over the tendency of the Galatians to return to the bondage of observing a pagan church year, of days and seasons. The growth of a pagen church year, cluttered with cash, is a sign of decreasing faith. Every Lord's Day is a celebration of the resurrection, and of the gift of the Spirit, of the incarnation in our street, and the crucifixion.

If religion will not save you, neither will irreligion. There is no intelligence in Sunday ball games, no culture in Sunday shows. Scientism is one of the most feebleminded of religions. Bernard Shaw noted "Every fool believes what his teacher tells him and calls his credulity science." Darwin led to Hitler and Stalin when he falsified facts to fortify his class of exploiters. Social Darwinism is a facade for robber barons. Russian Communism is far more evil than the church it replaced. The wars of science have murdered far more than wars of religion and invention has made revolt against tyranny almost impossible. Science has polluted and poisoned our world and has proven to be a false messiah.

It will do you no good to believe you have been given a base on balls unless you accept it by going to first base. If you do not put your foot on first base, your faith is useless. You believe in God? So does the devil. You believe the Bible is true? So does the devil, but he does not act on this belief, which is why he is a devil.

Faith is a personal relationship of trust. The implicit trust of my mother in Jesus is conclusive proof of the life eternal. Christian faith is living trust in Jesus. The real evidence that you are saved is that you live as a follower of Jesus.

> The dear Lord's best interpreters
> Are humble human souls
> The gospel of a life like hers.
> Is more than books or scrolls . . .
> The blessed Master none can doubt
> Revealed in human lives.

7

WITHOUT A SCORECARD

A scorecard makes it much easier to keep up with the game and who is doing what. The Christian has a scorecard which is also a rulebook and a record of past games. You cannot keep up with the game of living without the Word.

Authentic inspiration unlike any other volume breathes from its pages. It is unique in every sense. The Bible speaks to us where we are and of what we are and of what we ought to be. It finds us. There is inspiration in many writings but none comparable to this Word. Sacred books of religions contain many wise sayings but none is remotely like this volume. Moral compendia and treatises on theology are not in the same category with it. Those who read the newspaper instead of the Bible understand less of what is going on, as well as less of the past and the future.

> *We search the world for truth. We cull*
> *The good, the true, the beautiful,*
> *To find the best that has been said*
> *Is in the Book our mothers read.*

Its poetry furnishes insights beyond prosaic pedestrians who never look to the hills. Archaeological discoveries continue to validate its assertions and to dismay those who have tried to dispute its history. Its differing but harmonious accounts of incidents mark trustworthy witnesses. Our knowledge of most major events of the past depends on fewer writers. Here are many writers of several centuries, each writing in the language and revelation distinct to himself and yet furnishing a unified and comprehensive understanding of the external purpose in human life.

Diminutive mentalities unable to understand the great classics of the human soul, and to whom Milton and Browning are incomprehensible are unable to comprehend the Word. Puerile pedants who are unable to separate parts of a contemporary book written by different authors preen themselves on their ability to unravel Biblical books. Authorship and composition have no relation to inspiration and all this tedious misapprehension never accounts for the tremendous volume.

William Jennings Bryan, who by a change of less than 170,000 votes would have been elected president three times, noted that when a man says he does not believe in the Ten Commandments you had better watch your pocketbook. Naturally college presidents who exploit students do not want the Bible in their colleges; of course, professors with guilt complexes do not want their students confronted with the Word of God. Honest doubters are few, and if they are honest they will read the Book and no longer doubt. Most who profess not to believe it have never read it.

This Book is the basic document for knowledge of God, the perennial charter of human liberty. No other volume remotely approaches its influence in the past and no other so changes lives in the present. The Bible turned the hinges of history when it found men in the American Revolution which brought more progress in 2 centuries than in the previous 40 in government, science, invention, agriculture, business, Bible study.

The unsacramental untheological unecclesiastical Bible is the Book of the people, not the private possession of a priestly caste. Its best interpreters are humble souls and it is strength and light to them. Dictators from Babylon to China have hated this dangerous volume of personal and political redemption. It is a political volume and to eliminate its politics would cut out hundreds of its pages. It is much more dangerous to evil because it goes deeper to the roots of tyranny. It is the perennial opponent of pride, power and privilege and the friend of the poor, the neglected, the suffering. Those who read it stand up for human dignity as well as faith and are the first to resist totalitarian terror. The total impact of the Bible on the progress of nations is significant. "Let my people go" echoes from the volume to contemporary reformers. The Bible launched the revolution of the common man; it still frees slaves and brings the light of liberty to those who know it not, rescues brands from the burning, extinguishes the fires of hate, helps the victims and clears out the thieves from the Jericho road.

9

You will never know the score if you fail to study its pages. It will change your life, if you let it.

Life of ages, richly poured,
Love of God, unspent and free
Flow still in the prophets' word
And the people's liberty!

THE REAL WORLD SERIES

How large is your world? It is laughable when we call a contest between two teams, which until recent years was confined within the northeast, a World Series. The world of some people is a village, a small town, a little city, or a section of a city. We are told to go into all the world, but there are people whose world is between their home and their place of work. Are you local or long distance?

How large is the world beyond your vision? Do you speak the language of other people, follow their thought processes, read their literature? Or are you enclosed in a wall of one language? Do you think that all the world is like the high school to which you went? Do you reckon all colleges from one campus? What sort of mental furniture do you have? Is there in your mind any of the world of books, of which a lifetime can only afford a glimpse? Do you live in the fascinating and encouraging world of biography? The wisdom of the world is still in books. A life without books runs shallow.

How large is your world within? Do you live only for today? Or do you remember the yesterdays and plan for tomorrow? Have the years taught you much? Do you realize that you are part of the great flowing stream of history? If we do not know the history of the past, we will make the same old stupid mistakes again.

How large is the world above you? Do you have a faith that pierces beyond sun and stars? Is the Eternal most real to you? If Christ is in you and you are in Him, your world is unlimited. How large is your world?

It is because God has made a large universe for you and

a large world for you to dwell in, that God intends for you to live in love with your brothers. They are on the same team with you, or in the same league. What happens to them affects your standing. It takes their cooperation for you to win the pennant or even for you to get in the first division.

Galatians is very pointed about the truth the Word proclaims from Genesis to Revelation that God accepts no man as superior. God does not share our prejudices and our ignorance. He intends for us to treat all people as His children. In the second chapter of Galatians we read that the Apostle Peter was eating with Gentiles until some segregationists came up and he cowardly backed down. "You can't back down," he was informed by Brother Paul. If we segregate ourselves from Gentiles, most of the world will never hear our gospel; and it won't matter, because a gospel restricted to one group is not worth the world's hearing. The early church knew prejudices of creed and color, Greek and Barbarian, Jew and Gentile which make ours pale and insignificant, but there was one church for all. The Old Testament law was our conductor to lead us into this understanding. The New Testament gospel insists that God has made of one blood all races of men.

The liberty of the Christian man is a major theme of Galatians. "Where the Spirit of the Lord is, there is Liberty." The Christian man is under no human authority, political or ecclesiastical, unless that person has been chosen by the people and can be replaced by them if he becomes an overlord instead of a representative. Jesus allowed no hierarchy and pointed out the foolishness of allowing any to domineer over others and commanded "It shall not be so among you." No church which has any connection with Jesus can relinquish authority to officials. Bishops as shepherds of souls are Biblical; churches with any other bishops are outside the realm of Jesus.

Since God has accepted the man who trusts in Him, the man is equal to all in the sight of God. He was created equal. He is equal in that he is a sinner whose actions will always be tarnished by selfishness, from which none is exempt. He is endowed with inalienable rights, among which is liberty. We are not taught in school that because cruel Charlestonians and

11

greedy Bostonians sabotaged Thomas Jefferson's deep words against slavery out of the Declaration of Independence, we have been doomed to centuries of tragedy.

Liberty is not unregulated anarchy or *laissez faire* competition in which the ruthless drive others to the wall. Liberty for the train is to go on the track, liberty for the boat is to sail the water, liberty for the plane is to fly the air, liberty for the car is to move down the highway. Liberty is the possibility of being and doing the best. True liberty is to walk in the ways of God, "Whose service is perfect freedom."

A tremendous World Series is going on between those who believe in giving liberty and those who are determined to decide the destinies of others by dictatorship. In every land are some playing on either side, but some countries have more who prefer liberty. Democracy is harder because it requires the majority to take some part, to do some thing. It is much easier to succumb to dictatorship. Slavery in a totalitarian state today is worse than slavery of the past because of the devices science has tragically furnished for brainwashing, spying, murdering. The slave of a century ago was not enslaved every waking moment to flickers impelling him to greed, hate, lust and more slavery. The American spirit is in the old spiritual

> *Rather than be a slave*
> *I'll be buried in my grave,*
> *And go home to be with God.*

We fought a world series for liberty in 1775, 1812, 1917, 1941. As Christians we have to stand against the slavery of dictators. The extreme Left and extreme Right meet as in a circle. The real choice is between Above and Below. Communists and loud anti-Communists join in smearing those who stand for liberty. On the last page of *Animal Farm* the pigs and profiteers join together.

The longest World Series has been going on since the Garden of Eden and involves every land, every age, every life. There is a story that some foolish boys decided to scare members of a country church and dressed up as the devil. When they climbed in a window, the members rushed out the door. One old sister could barely hobble and she felt the devil breathing over her shoulder. She turned around and pleaded, "Please, Mr. Devil, I've been talking against you in this church for 50 years, but, really, I've been on your side all the time."

Who is on the Lord's side?

HOW YOU PLAY SHOWS WHAT YOU ARE

The home run in the ninth inning is spectacular, but the man who hits it may have done little else all season. One good play does not make you a good player. The relief pitcher who strikes out six straight and wins the game may not have won another game. It is not what you do in one game, but your average through the season that counts. The papers print the baseball averages because they show what kind of a player he is from day to day. A player is judged by his batting, fielding, and pitching average. The way you play most of the time shows what you are.

You give yourself away unconsciously. Your speech tells what is on your mind, and what is not. Your ways advertise your inner character. A tree is known by its fruits. You get few peaches from apple trees, and few persimmons from pine trees. You cannot make a Christmas tree into an orange tree by tying oranges on it. You can't become good by picking up a few good habits; goodness has to come from within. A change in inner character is necessary, not just the addition or subtraction of a few habits. It is not doing evil things which makes you evil; it is because you are evil that you do evil things. You cannot get to be good just by doing good things; if you are good, you will naturally do good things. These are not perfectionist rules; you may be good on the average, and do some bad things, or you may be bad on the average and do some good things as an exception. You are not saved because you love your neighbor; you love your neighbor because you have been saved by Christ from your selfishness.

The fifth chapter of Galatians contains a list of the sins which it says that those who practice shall not inherit the kingdom of God. This is the passage of which Robert Browning wrote:

> *There's a text within Galatians,*
> *Once you slip on it, entails*
> *Twenty-nine distinct damnations,*
> *One sure if the other fails.*

God warns that those who commit these sins brutalize, paralyze, and destroy their inner being. The list begins with sins of immorality among the married and the unmarried, which are in every such list in the Bible. God made the family the basis of human society and these sins break down the family. God created the home as the center of living and these sins wreck the home. Lust is the murder of the soul.

Within half a century we have gone from the most Puritanical of peoples to the opposite. Impuritanism is the surest way to destroy a people. The profound Spanish philosopher, Miguel Unamuno, observed, "Lust, gambling and drunkenness stultify a man. If for every school which is opened, a gambling den, a house of vice and a bar are not closed, the school is useless."

No people have ever been exposed to more incitements to lust. Filthy novels, magazines and TV programs break down moral standards. God demands decency in dress instead of imitation of the marks of evil women. Will Rogers noted long ago that if education did not destroy the movies, the submoronic movies would destroy education. No one comes out of a movie as pure as he went in, while drive-ins are dens of sordid shame. Movies demoralize youth and age and sabotage faith and love. Adult movies means adulterous movies; films are no longer run to make money as much as to provide perverts and prostitutes. Those who let their children see this garbage and those who allow others to see it are guilty in the sight of God. Those who look, listen, allow, and participate, shut themselves out of the pure world of God. They just do not know Jesus.

Sorcery, which is addiction to narcotics, superstition, astrology, purchasable religion, all the means of keeping from the responsibility of being human are also sins which shut out from the commonwealth of God. Alcohol is one of the quickest ways to dehumanize people, and drunkenness excludes from the realm of God. Drunkenness is a major factor in murder, crime, lust; it is the destruction of human personality. It turns human beings into murderous maniacs, fills slums with misery, and suburbs with sorrow. God has no forgiveness for those who sell poison, insanity and murder by the bottle, or who help it to be sold. Saintly Cardinal Leger insists, "90% of man's misery comes from alcohol."

Murder is taking away the life of another. Only God has the right to take life, as only He can create it. But God has commanded men to take away the lives of those who murder, or otherwise murderers could destroy the human race. Those who would allow only murderers to inflict capital punishment are acting feeblemindedly. Human life never was cheaper and thousands are murdered every day. Hundreds of murders are on our screens every day and incitements to violence are unceasing. God has eternal death for merchants of death.

Greed and hate freeze human life until it disappears. These are more respectable sins but just as deadly. Millions worship idols of cash and statues, power and pride. Disloyalty to the Spirit of God is shown by malice and spite, meanness and quarreling, strife and selfishness. Keeping up with the Joneses is deadly to the soul. Heresy is the sin of sectarianism, imagining that a splinter is truth, and trying to restrict the Eternal to a narrow sect. The envious can forgive anything except those leading better lives and with grim stubbornness they smear those with more intelligence and better character. The Bible makes clear that hate is murder and no murderer has eternal life.

These words of Galatians make clear that those who practice these sins are lost to themselves and to God. It is strange that you never heard this passage preached on; this is the major catalog of mortal sins in the New Testament, although it is no different from the message from Exodus to Revelation.

Because they have professed faith in Christ, millions are misled into imagining that this passage does not apply to them, but it was written to church members to remind them that faith shows itself in life and those who commit these sins are lost. God will forgive anyone who repents of any of these sins. God will forgive again and again. One who commits murder can be forgiven when he repents. But if he keeps on murdering, he is clearly not a child of God. Those who continue in these sins will never see heaven. "Narrow is the way to life, and few are finding it," said Jesus.

Those who love God try to walk in His ways. The Christian may never reach in this world the perfection of loving his neighbor as himself, but he will not practice these mortal sins. God will give strength to escape them. We live in the Spirit in grateful love for the love of God in Christ which redeemed us from ourselves and from our sins. It is harder to do than to say, and harder to be than to do. But how we live shows what we are. The fruits of the Spirit mark those who are in the Spirit: love, joy, peace, patience, gentleness, goodness, faith, meekness, temperance.

THERE IS AN UMPIRE

An umpire is essential to a ball game. The umpire is more often right. He is in a better position to see and to know. The fan in the farthest bleacher can not see as much as the man behind the plate. By years of experience the umpire learns to tell a ball from a strike, a safe from an out. He makes mistakes, but not as many as you may think.

Job voiced the hope that there is an Eternal Umpire. There is One and He always calls them right. He calls nothing arbitrarily, but through the choices of our lives. You sow what you reap and you find what you seek. "Sow a thought and you reap a deed; sow a deed and you reap a habit; sow a habit and you reap a character; sow a character and you reap a destiny."

There must be justice in the universe. The evil clearly are not punished in this world. Those who make this world a hell for others make themselves a hell forever. Children are not as afraid of hell as they are afraid there is not a hell for the brutes and bullies who wreck boyhood and girlhood days. Hell is remorse, isolation with evil, separation from God and from all that is good. Fire is a symbol. All words are symbols, but they denote realities beyond the symbols. The gentle Jesus spoke more of hell than any other Biblical speaker. Hell is not for the kind, not for the humble, not for the repentant, not for those who fail to dot an "i" and cross a "t" theologically, and not for those who look to God in trust.

A generation ago it was easy to see that there had to be a hell for Hitler, Stalin, Mussolini. There was no adequate punishment possible in this world for those who tried to wipe out a whole people with scientific exactitude. Just as cruel men are in power today.

There has to be a hell for those who burn babies alive, for those who wage germ warfare and poison reservoirs, for profiteering merchants of death, for manufacturers of inflammable clothes for babies and of explosive toys for children. And for dictators feeding prisoners to sharks, senators letting children of God suffocate in coal mines, governors getting rich selling out adolescents to drunkenness and delirium tremens, cruel politicians stirring up hate and greed. There is a hell for those who torture the helpless, who abuse the insane, who exploit helpless women, for professors who exult in wrecking morals, for deans who pervert students, for those who drown weary old peons in Georgia swamps. There has to be a place for evangelists who betray the gospel and for arrogant bishops and mean laymen who loll in luxury while they let children be bitten by rats in shanty rectories, who drive ministers to nervous breakdowns, break the hearts of their wives, wreck their ministries and poison the water of life. Those who by screen and print incite daily to cruel lust, murder, hate, greed will be given the verdicts they deserve.

It is because God loves that He warns against the things that hurt you. Hate destroys the inner fibre of being. Hate

17

disintegrates the human personality. Hate blinds and cripples and dwarfs. Hate gradually blackens all the horizons of living. Who lives in hate is in hell now. Lust, cruelty, greed do the same. Hell is in some faces now. No man was ever sent to hell; he sends himself there by making himself a part of hell.

"Be not deceived; God is not mocked; whatsoever a man soweth, that shall he also reap." This is true now, and forever. "Babe" Ruth said that he changed his way of living when he realized that he as well as those above him had to account to God. At the heart of the universe is eternal justice and mercy. In this we trust as we try to turn others away from the evils which bring their inevitable harvest.

The compassion of Jesus is as eternal as His justice. "The bruised reed He will not break." He is the Healer of broken hearts. Those whom the Umpire calls safe are safe forever. Safe on the other shore are those who served the purpose of God in their generation. "And so He brings them to their desired haven."

God is not unfaithful, to forget our labors of love. The Eternal Umpire will reward for every kind word, every good deed, every act of mercy. Even the best we do is so inadequate that we need "our good and ill alike forgiven." Our loving Father accepts our imperfect attempts to help others, our good intentions often frustrated by those we try to aid. Our eternal mansions are built from what we have sent ahead. "Eye has not seen, neither has ear heard, neither has it entered into the heart of man what good things God has prepared for those who love Him."

DON'T DIE ON THIRD!

The world is like a baseball diamond. You may get to first base by your own efforts, or by a base on balls given you. You may be sacrificed to second base by parents and friends. You may get to third base on a hit by someone else, or by an error of the opposition. In baseball, you have to depend on others to get you home, as well as on yourself. In life, it depends on you whether you get home. You can not stay on third base and do any good for the team; you have to get home.

To get tired of doing good is to die on third base. It is easy to get tired of doing good, and to follow the line of least resistance. You can decide that there is no use trying to make a crop, because the rain will ruin it, or the drought. Age or weariness may tempt you to get tired of doing good.

Our world is discouraging in the revolt against intelligence, in minds as empty as a school in July smearing all who read. Some feel inferior if you make them think. Our public and private life is poisoned by hatred of intelligence.

The fact that you are discouraged may be a good sign. Vegetables are never discouraged. Discouragement may show that you are thinking. Discouragement may be realistic wisdom. It is good that I do not have to be 20 again, and know as little as I did then. Youth believes it can get by with everything; age knows it has never gotten away with anything.

There is enough goodness in the world that sin is still news. Crime is still worth putting in headlines, because it is unusual. Suppose you read headlines like these: "Honest Bank Cashier Discovered," "Loving Mother Found in Community," "Business Man Reported to Pay His Debts," "Married Couple Still Happy." If we had such headlines, it would mean that goodness is rare. Our emotional insecurity comes in part from living in headlines of evil.

The tide will turn. A man who made his first political race in 1757 lost the horse traders by denouncing their stealing, lost the saloon keepers by trying to close their liquor shops and lost the church vote by false rumors that those criminals spread. That wasn't the end of him; the fellow's name was George Washington. Another man a few years later refused to buy drinks for voters and was defeated for the legislature. You may have heard of him; his name was James Madison.

God is still eternal and all powerful. The God of love is a more powerful force than hate. We have to learn to see things through even when we can not see through things.

Discouragement can be cured by bearing the burdens of others. Some burdens each one must bear for himself, others

19

we can share. When we share, a new radiance comes into living. If we do good, as we have opportunity, to all men, and especially to those who share our faith in God, we shall not have much time for discouragement. We need not get tired of well doing. We must not give up fighting against all kinds of evil.

The farmer has faith that the crop will come up. It is not our religion but our faith which overcomes the world. We shall reap as we have sown: cotton from cotton, corn from corn, evil from evil, goodness from goodness. Who sows only to this life reaps only in this life; who sows to the spirit reaps in a harvest without end. Our redemption is a surrender to the Christ who is always and everywhere present. Keep up the fight—you may be essential for victory!

> *Say not the struggle naught availeth,*
> *The labor and the wounds are vain,*
> *The enemy faints not nor faileth,*
> *And as things have been, so they will remain.*
>
> *If hopes were dupes, it may be fears are liars;*
> *It may be in yon smoke concealed*
> *Your comrades chase even now the fliers,*
> *And, but for you, possess the field.*
>
> *For while the tired waves breaking*
> *Seem here no painful inch to gain,*
> *Far back, through creeks and inlets making,*
> *Comes silent, flooding in the main.*
>
> *And not through eastern windows only*
> *When daylight comes, comes in the light,*
> *Eastward the sun comes slowly, slowly,*
> *But westward look, the land is bright.*

A SACRIFICE WILL WIN

A sacrifice hit is the finest play in baseball. You deliberately make an out, so that another man on your side can get a base farther. It is hard to train players to make sacrifice hits; they like the glory of making hits for themselves. They prefer to get on base themselves, rather than to help someone else score a run. A few years ago a league playoff was decided when a sacrifice in the ninth inning tied the score, and a second sacrifice brought in the pennant-winning run.

Always some in the family sacrifice that the others may have more. Some sacrifice themselves by running for office that another may be elected, or for principle, realizing they will lose, but that the cause will win. Some let others have the glory for what they have done in the church, or hold remote forts in order that the victory of the cause may be sure.

> *If I have been perverse or cruel or cold;*
> *If I have sought safe shelter in the fold,*
> *When Thou hast given me some fort to hold,*
> *Dear Lord, forgive!*

The apostle Paul could have been proud of being a member of the people to whom God had given His fullest revelation, and of being a citizen of the great empire which had brought peace and order to much of the world, whose legions tramped its paved roads from Scotland to Galatia. He could have been proud of his education at Tarsus and at the school of Gamaliel in Jerusalem, of his remarkable intelligence as one of the greatest geniuses of the human race, or his strange experience on the Damascus road, the like of which was granted to no other. He could have gloried in his achievements in spreading the gospel where it had never been heard and his sufferings, which he lists in Second Corinthians. He was too wise and too Christian to be proud of any of these.

The cross has been the center of human history from the day Jesus died upon it. The One who died upon it has been the motive power behind multitudes who have walked this earthly path since that day. The cross was a personal relationship between Paul and Christ. By Christ, the world was crucified to him, and he to the world. He walked the way of the cross. He bore himself the marks of the Lord Jesus.

You are not a Christian unless you are crucified. You are not a Christian unless you are despised, unless you are criticized. Jesus said that no one was doing right when all spoke well of

21

him. You are not a Christian unless you are ridiculed by some and hated by others for speaking the truth and doing the right. You are not a Christian unless you have been neglected and ignored, in community, in school, in state, in business, in organizations, even in church, because you sincerely try to follow Jesus. Until you are lied about, until you are kept from bringing your message and your life to those who need it, you are not in the way of the cross. One of the most certain ways the world persecutes is to keep you from positions where others could learn from you. For there is no answer to a Christian life, and you could not be lied about to those who knew your sincerity even in your mistakes. You are not a Christian until you are persecuted by some religious people as well as by other thieves.

Jesus said, "If any man will come after me, he must disregard himself and take up his cross day by day, and follow Me." There is no cheaper rate for being a Christian, there is no easier way. Christ crucified for you and in you is incomplete until you are crucified with Him. It is not suffering that makes you a Christian; it is because you are a Christian that you suffer such persecution. Don't you want to walk in the way of the cross that leads home?

> *When I survey the wondrous cross*
> *On which the Prince of glory died,*
> *My richest gain I count but loss,*
> *And pour contempt on all my pride.*
>
> *Forgive it, Lord, that I should boast,*
> *Save in the death of Christ, my God;*
> *All the vain things that charm me most,*
> *I sacrifice them to His blood.*
>
> *See from His head, His arms, His feet,*
> *Sorrow and love flow mingled down;*
> *Did e'er such love and sorrow meet,*
> *Or thorns compose so rich a crown?*
>
> *Were the whole realm of nature mine,*
> *That were a present far too small;*
> *Love so amazing, so divine,*
> *Demands my soul, my life, my all.*

The sacrifice has been made; you can come home.

26,000 DAYS TO LIVE

So teach us to number our days, that we may apply our hearts unto wisdom.

Psalm 90:12

Twenty-six thousand days to live. That is what you have if you are an average American. A few years ago the average American lived to be 59 years old; now the average man lives to be 67, the average woman to 72. If you are 70 now, you will live, if you are average, 17 more years; if you are 60, 25 more years, if you are 40, 32 years more. If you have a baby girl a year old, she has over 80 years ahead of her, and your baby boy has almost that much. The Bible says that the days of our years were intended by God to be three score and ten, and we are practically there in this country. What shall we do with these days? How shall we number them?

There are 3,600 Sundays in an average life now. Think of the opportunities to worship God in church more than 3,000 Sundays! If you miss worship then, you can never recover that Sabbath; it is gone forever. A Sunday of several services enriches life. You have thousands of opportunities in your life of worshipping by radio. The Lord's Day is an opportunity for visiting the sick and the needy, for going to see family and friends, for reading, and for listening to spiritual music. Sunday is a good time for the Bible study for which so many fail to find time on other days. Sundays as days of rest, of withdrawal from the work and pleasures of the week, are a great help to mind and body and soul. Sundays can be a golden memory.

You spend one-third of your life in sleeping; you sleep 8,000 days. Sleep is one of the great gifts of God. The psalmist writes: "He giveth his beloved sleep," and the writer of wisdom noted: "The sleep of a laboring man is sweet." Those who work hard have less difficulty with sleeping. Trust in the Lord and He will give you sleep and rest. Sleeping in church is not a good habit, but people could be asleep in worse places; if you fall asleep, you probably need it. A great deal of foolishness and sin is committed by people who are not awake enough to know what they are doing; lack of sleep is a form of intoxication.

Many of our leaders would do less foolish things if they slept enough; students would do better work if they slept more. Sleeping a little longer may make you able to work harder and think clearer while you are awake.

You will probably spend 8,000 days of your 26,000 in work, including the years of education to prepare for work. That is as it should be. Man was created to work as well as to rest. We need not work our bodies six full days, but we need to work our minds. One idle drone is too many. God Himself is a Worker, and His Son worked as a Carpenter when He was here on earth. To work at your job is a good way to spend one-third of your days. Each of us needs to contribute his or her part to the world's work. If you are well enough to work, and strong enough, you should be able to find some task which will interest you. Going to and from work, cleaning up and so forth, takes about 4,000 days more, and eating takes 2,000 days. Eating is not a bad habit, though overeating or undereating is.

This leaves us just 4,000 days. All people have to sleep and eat and work, and their lives are much alike in these ways. What we do in the other 4,000 days is what makes our lives. Our lives are colored by what we do in these days. What can you do with 4,000 days? They sound like a lot of time, but actually as the days come, they rush by. Out of these 4,000 days comes our time for recreation. How you play may be more revealing of your inner self than how you work, for your job may not be of your choosing, but your recreation can be. John Milton expressed a forgotten strength of Puritanism when he wrote of refraining from work for recreation.

And when God sends a cheerful hour, refrain.

Out of these 4,000 days comes our time for worship, for Bible and other reading, for listening to good music, for writing letters and for community improvement. These are days for gaining culture, making friends, wandering in the hills, gazing at the stars. Be sure that you number these 4,000 days that they may be filled with what makes life richer.

Moses in the 90th psalm gives his conclusions to numbering

our days. The beauty of the Lord God will be upon us. Life will be beautiful, if we live as the Lord asks us to live, if we number our days with wisdom, and use them in His joyful service. And He will establish the work of our hands. The deeds we do, do not last except as they are built into the lives of others. Our unselfish influence will be here long after we have gone. The principles and institutions into which we give our best will bear the results of our work. We pray God to carry on whatever of good we may have done, and we know that if we mark our days with the beauty of His ways, our work can never end. And so may we number our days in this year, and may our plans and purposes which are in His will be fulfilled, and may the beauty of the Lord Jesus be upon us all, this year, and evermore.

NOBODY KNOWS THE TROUBLE
I'VE SEEN

"Nobody knows what I have been through." Have you ever said that? "No one has ever had the problems I have." Have you ever felt that way? "I am the only one to whom this has happened." "Nobody can understand because no one has been through what I have." Do you believe that? A spiritual says, "Nobody knows the trouble I've seen." You are mistaken. In the words of I Corinthians 10:13, "There has no temptation taken you but such as is common to man."

Are you tempted to think that your sickness is unlike any one else's? Go see a doctor and tell him of your peculiar health problems and he will diagnose your problem from a book of such cases: it may be so common that there is a whole volume on it; he may will you a standard prescription, worked out for others with the same trouble. Boys in the army almost fainted when told they had a herpes simplex or catarrhus conjunctivitis, but recovered when they found out these were common ailments. You are not the only one whose health is a problem; do not be tempted to despair of your health.

You are not the first to face the temptation of youth, of age, of middle age. You are not the only one who has the temptation to worry. Worry is lack of faith, worrying can not possibly help you, only hurt you. "Take your burden to the Lord and leave it there."

The temptation to be unfaithful to your wife or husband is the same others have. Do not fool yourself: "I am different"; you are not. "My wife doesn't understand me"; maybe the trouble is that she does understand you. "I can't live like other folks"; but you are like them. They have the same temptations. There is the temptation to break up the family because of certain problems and quarrels. Books can tell you the standard disagreements in marriage, and how quarrels can be used constructively.

You may have the temptation of lying; others have it. You may be tempted to give up fighting against evil; others get weary in well doing. When you are tempted to give in to sorrow, remember that no life has ever been lived without tragedy. If you are tempted by alcoholism, remember that thousands have fought this temptation and have overcome it, and many are willing to help you overcome this giant of sin.

Are you tempted to doubt? Ministers have heard more doubts than you have. Doubts come to all people, but they are not the end. Honest doubt is honest only if it seeks an answer to its questions.

Are you tempted to discouragement over present conditions, to growing cold? or do you realize that similar conditions have prevailed after many wars? The high stealing and low morals which followed our Revolution were succeeded by religious awakening and Jeffersonian Democracy. The postwar letdown after 1812 was succeeded by the missionary movement and Jacksonian reform. The gilded age after the War between the States which knew no culture and wanted no worship except of the almighty dollar was succeeded by social preaching and the political evangelism of Bryan and Wilson.

Our golden age came in the Wilson administration with confidence, hope, peace and progress. The American people evinced more political intelligence in 1912 than since; even the most backward candidate for president was more constructive than any his party has named since then. Critical exposure of social evils was diminishing them. The best seller was *The Inside of the Cup,* in which a minister led in reforming a city.

After World War I came brazenly dishonest administrations, a demoralizing screen and press, the evaporation of the Sabbath to submoronic entertainment and religion tailored to cash contributors. The New Deal was a partial recovery from this and then World War II shattered much of the strength of our life and the Cold War continued this. The worst things about wars are what come after them and the aftermath of the worst war was the worst.

The Venerable Bede, writing in the 8th century about the aftermath of a war with the Picts, observed

> When, however, the ravages of the enemy at length ceased, the island began to abound with such plenty of grain as had never been known in any age before; with plenty, luxury increased and this was immediately attended with all sorts of crimes, in particular, cruelty, hatred of truth and love of falsehood; insomuch that if anyone among them happened to be inclined to truth, all the rest abhorred and persecuted him, as if he had been an enemy of his country.

You can learn that others have gone through the same experiences you have by reading deep books. You can discover it by perusing the pages of history. You can find it out from the experiences of others. You can see your own problems mirrored in the pages of the Bible. And you can learn of the meaning of life from Jesus. "Nobody knows the trouble I've seen; nobody knows but Jesus."

Our text goes on: "God is faithful." You can depend on Him, and He will show a way out from every temptation. There is a difference between faith that carries you and a religion you have to carry. God is no heavy burden, but the One who will share our burdens. Church-going may be something we feel we ought to do, or strength for the days to come. Bible reading can be a task, or food for daily growth. Prayer can become not a duty but fresh air, communion not a requirement but a window for the grace of God to enter. God's hold on us is greater than

27

our hold on Him. The soul that on Jesus leans for repose is assured that He is faithful forevermore. He will never, no, never, no, never, forsake!

WE LIVE IN TWO DIFFERENT WORLDS

You belong to this world; I do not belong to this world.

John 8:23

These words of Jesus remind us: we live in two different worlds. There are those who live in the outward world of sight and sound and sensation. There are others who live beyond this outer world in an inward world to which the things which are seen are trivial, but the things which are unseen are everlasting. Those who live only by the outward are unable to understand those who live by the inward. We live in two different worlds.

There are those who live by the material; to them money and ranch houses and Cadillacs and expensive display are the important things. They miss the meaning of life. Those who live by the spiritual do not ignore the material world of food and shelter, but to them it is secondary compared with the world of the spirit. Those with a birthright in the realm of the spirit are unconcerned with standards which judge the worth of a man or a woman by money and conspicuous waste. To the world of the spiritual the computation of success by adding together what one gets rather than what one gives is very foolish. What a man is worth is not what he owns. A Christian is one who does not know how to succeed. He is much in silence. He is not a slave to sinister shadows on a screen. The others live in a world of illusion; we live in the world of reality.

And we live in two different worlds, of man or of God. There are those who take the easy way out, who give up for appearances' sake, who ally themselves with any evil. Those who live in the world of God are not concerned with what people think of them. They dress by sense, not by style. They can not accept the tawdry standards of man or of any human organization. They live in the highland air of God and its free breezes, bow to no Baal and bend to no smooth compromise with sin. For what God thinks is all that matters, and what God wills shall prevail, if it breaks every habit and tradition and custom of man.

This is the devil's world. He told Jesus that it was his and that he gives it to whom he wishes. The devil is a liar, but not completely. He does control the world in the evil sense of the world order. It is evident that he is the prince of this world. Look who gets to the top in government, in finance, in business, in education, in religion, in publicity, and in popularity. Whose names are trumpeted and shown around the earth? Not the men of God. So rarely does a good man even become known to his generation that we are apt to suspect if he does that he has either sold out or that the devil is tempting him to sell out. Those whom the world praises owe their souls to the company store.

None of the rulers of this world knew the Lord of glory when they crucified Him. They crucified Him because of willful blindness. They knew no better because they wanted to know no better. So Jeremiah and Paul witnessed of their generations. Jefferson said that 15 of 16 who got to the top were rogues and scoundrels; things do not seem to have changed much. If you doubt it, look at presidents and governors, vice-presidents and senators, generals and editors, commentators and columnists, college presidents and bishops.

It is written of the Roman soldiers around the cross: "So they took the money and did as they were told." Here, a few verses before the Great Commission, is the Great Omission. They could have been the first Christian witnesses, but they sold out.

> *I was a Roman soldier in my prime;*
> *Now age is on me, and the yoke of time.*
> *I saw your risen Christ, for I am he*
> *Who reached the hyssop to Him on the tree;*
> *And I am one of the two who watched beside*
> *The sepulchre of Him we crucified.*

29

Years have I wandered, carrying my shame;
Now let the tooth of time blot out my name.
For we, who all the wonder might have told,
Kept silence, for our mouths were stopped with gold.

This poem of Edwin Markham reminds us that there are laymen and ministers who sell out and do as they are told. Like those in Acts who were angry when they saw their hope of gain was gone, they fight those who live in the world of the spirit.

The reader of the Bible lives in another world, breathes a different air. He is never certain where he will be a year from now nor what he may be doing but he knows the Lord will lead him. He understands the medieval Irish monks who launched their boat into the channel and threw the oars away, confident God would guide them where He willed. He may not be quite this much of a quietist but each day he does the little he can do and leaves the rest to the Eternal. He has learned that all things work together for good to those who love God. He knows from life as from the Word that God's eternal pattern is inclusive and conclusive. The world in which he lives is a world of serenity and trust.

Our world is honest and true. We who live in it are not 100% honest or true but we try to live more honestly and more truthfully every day through the power of Him who loves us. We know when we have failed and we ask forgiveness to walk daily in newness of life. The world passes away but we who do the will of God abide forever.

WHY DO SUCH THINGS HAPPEN TO ME?

O the depth of the riches both of the wisdom and knowledge of God! How unsearchable are His judgments, and His ways past finding out! For of Him, and through Him, and to Him, are all things: to whom be glory for ever.

Romans 11:33,36

Why do such things happen to you and to me? Why does God let them happen? Why does God let things happen to the world that are so tragic and terrible? Is there any explanation? Why should failure and disappointment and suffering and sorrow come to us?

It would be wrong to say that all of these come from God. There is in the world human sin, which is responsible for much that is wrong. But even apart from this there is much about life that just does not make sense. Perhaps we do not understand.

There is something fundamentally wrong with human life. Much of human life we do not understand. It is possible that God has purposes about our lives which can not be clear to us. His purposes for mankind are above our understanding. His ways, unsearchable and past finding out.

But there are still in human life problems and evils which can not be accounted for by referring them to the mystery of God's purposes. The good God made a good world. He certainly did not intend sickness, toil, sorrow, death, as part of His plan. It is a libel on God to say that He intended to have these. It is unfair to God to blame Him for the human body as it is after centuries of misuse. The evil in us and around us can not be the will or desire of the good God.

The third chapter of Genesis is picture writing, but a picture is never as full or as deep as what it represents. This picture of original human life has deeps in it far below the surface of the words. They are deeps which we plumb only so far as life drives us to.

God made man upright. He was made in the image of God and to grow more like Him. Man was given everything to enjoy. But his pride lifted him up, and he desired to become as God. This temptation to make self the center of the universe was too strong for him, and the result was what is called The Fall. Since then man has toiled against wind and weeds and weather, and work has been his lot. Creative work is of God, but toil is not. The Fall also resulted in the lowering of woman to a subordinate position, with inequality, pain, and the confused relation between the sexes which bewilders us today. And death came into human

31

life and remains there. God meant man to live forever with Him without any death.

Every small garden bears in its weeds a token of the Fall. Every great empire bears in its cruelties the same token. The life of a nation is marked by pride and failure for the same reason. Your own personal life suffers from failure to fulfill itself likewise. Human nature is warped. It is not incapable of good, but it is bent away from good. This is even more evident in the headlines of a morning paper than in any sermon.

The Fall is not a doctrine of sadness; it is a doctrine of hope. Chesterton has called it the good news of original sin. Christianity does not end with fallen man, it gives that as an explanation of the world and of human life. It does not say that human life is as God intended. It does not say that your life is as God intended. But it does say that God intends a new world, a new humanity, and a new life for you. And it provides a Redeemer in Jesus who gives us that new life now, that new world in the future.

The wisdom of God is far beyond us. God's ways are not our ways. God is so much greater than we can dream. There is no depth to the riches of His understanding. All of our knowledge added together is just a drop in the ocean of His knowledge.

Ride through the woods and look at the hundreds of shades and tints upon the trees. God is a lover of color. Look at the hundreds of kinds of leaves and flowers and plants. It takes a whole lifetime to study just a few of them. God knows all about them. Study the stars. You can spend a whole lifetime on astronomy, and you will be thinking some of God's thoughts after Him. Study the minerals, and you will find the many different varieties God has made. His ways are unsearchable.

When Job was distressed by his suffering which he did not understand, God gave him a curious answer. God did not tell him why he was suffering or explain the divine purpose. Instead God called Job's attention to the hippopotamus. God said: "Job. You wouldn't have made a hippopotamus; you don't see any reason for having one; but I do, and that ought to be a lesson to you that I have purposes beyond your understanding." God went on to tell Job that if even the animals around us reveal more of God than we understand, we ought not to expect to understand all His ways with us. A visit to a zoo can be a profound spiritual experience. When you look at all of the animals, looking as curious to us as we look to them, you wonder why the Lord made some of them. I would have left some of them out of my world; so would you. Their presence shows that God has other thoughts than ours. The God revealed in biology is a great God and much different from man.

God's judgments are unsearchable, as His ways are past finding out. History yields as many riddles as nature. Neither speaks with a clear voice. Why does this nation rise and that nation fall? Why does this movement fail and that conspiracy succeed? Why do some characters play large parts and others of greater abilities just edge into the scene? The study of history is humbling to human pride. It does not give sure and easy answers. Why doesn't God stop wars? Why doesn't He end injustice? Why doesn't He help us in our good intentions and high plans? The answer is again that God's purposes are so much above ours that we can not understand many of them.

We can understand this: that all things come from Him. He is the source, the only source of all life. From Him all things come, seen and unseen, understood and misunderstood. There is nothing that He did not make. He made the universe and all that is therein. He made the mind and all that is therein. He made the heart and all that we have and all that we are to be.

All things are through Him. In Him we live and move and have our being. He is not far from each one of us. He sustains by His mighty power the rock and the waterfall, the bird and the electron, the rose and the man next door. If He failed to uphold all things by the word of His power, the universe would crash. Like some cosmic law of gravitation, He holds all things together. We are "within the circle of God's love," as Phillipps', the most beautiful of modern translations, expresses it.

All things are to Him. He is the end of all our striving. He is the goal of the whole creative process. He is the fulfillment of our highest hopes. He leads all of His creation toward that far off, divine event to which the whole of life leads. He is beginning and ending, the Alpha and Omega, the first and the last. And in His final victory is the assurance of our hope. How unsearchable are His judgments, and His ways past finding out. For Him, and through Him, and to Him are all things: to whom be glory for ever.

FOLLOW THE SIGNS

You don't get more gas unless you think you need it. The poor in spirit are blessed because they know they need something. Those who feel life is as good as can be are hopeless. Those who think they are well can not be healed; those who think they know cannot learn; those who think they are perfect can not be saved. Heaven is for those who feel their spiritual need.

Some signs on the highway of life are expected, some are not. Wait for the green light. It will turn, though it may take a long time. You may have to wait all your life but the mourners are the only ones who can be comforted. True mourners are concerned with the evil and suffering of human society, with its ignorance and indifference. We are not Buddhists seeking peace of mind or isolationists. Mourning is shown by justice and mercy to all.

Did you ever ride in an old wagon and feel the hard wooden wheels resist every bump, every rock, every hole in the road? You do not feel these if you ride on rubber tires, for the rubber gives in rather than resisting. Meekness is not weakness; it is giving in and going on. Moses was very meek but very strong. Let others run over you. Overlook offenses. Accept little places. "He that is down need fear no fall, He that is low no pride."

Get on the right road and stay on it. Did you ever get on an unmarked detour? The right road is the road of right, of righteousness, of justice. It is not the road of empty ceremonial but of being right in the sight of God and right to our neighbor. In every nation he that fears God and does justice is acceptable to the Eternal. Whoever is hungry and thirsty for personal and social righteousness is on the right road.

Drive carefully; the life you save may be your own. Only the merciful can receive mercy because they have rain barrels.

God sends mercy on all, but only the merciful can take it. The kind can understand the kindness of God. Mercy to the merciless is unmerciful; we must not let them injure others. Mercy may require force to prevent the unmerciful exploiting others.

Keep your windshield clean. You can not see God through a muddy windshield. What can muddy the windshield of life? Many novels, magazines, movies, tv programs darken our vision. God did not give us eyes to see such. One cleaning is not enough; it is a daily task. Even a "Drive Safely" sign can block the windshield; religion becoming an end in itself may block the way to God. Kierkegaard said: "Purity of heart is to will one thing." "To be physically minded is death, but to be spiritually minded is life and peace."

You need more oil to overcome the friction of life. Wars of class, sex, age and youth, town and country, nation and nation, need peace. God calls peacemakers His children; the world has harder names for them. The peacemaker must oppose militarism spending so much of our money and our lives, must oppose the idea that war is inevitable, must help bring peace between races, churches, groups, nations, persons.

Follow the signs; the road is marked. The persecuted are rewarded with exceeding joy. No one is a Christian who does not suffer persecution. Unless you are crucified in some way, you are not following Jesus. He said that the way of the cross is inescapable for His followers. Only a life built on the cross is built for eternity.

The straight and narrow road is marked with signs. This marker is for Moses, enduring persecution from the ungrateful and ignorant people to whom he gave his life. This is for Joshua, almost murdered for daring to point the way to the land of promise. That is for Micaiah, daring to tell the unwelcome truth although outnumbered 400 to 1. That is for Amos indicting the rich and the rulers with God's demand for justice. Isaiah, a great soul of compassion and courage, is murdered for his concern for faith and for the poor. Jeremiah's life is marked by persecution because of his sincere love of his people. John the Forerunner is murdered for exposing the sin of a ruler. Paul is stoned, imprisoned, finally murdered, for his faith. John is a slave exiled to the lead mines of Patmos when he sees his visions of the ultimate triumph of truth.

The road is marked, with millions of markers of those who followed in His train. Latimer burns to set a light aflame, Savonarola because he preached sincerity and decency to Florence. Wesley defies bishops and mobs to bring the gospel to the common man. An endless list could be made of the markers on the royal road of the holy cross. A good life is far more offensive to the evil than good words. A Puritan is uncomfortable to have around because he is confirmed by conscience.

Woodrow Wilson, the saintliest and most intellectual of presidents, was bitterly persecuted. World peace was wrecked by jealous Republicans to hurt him but it hurt the world more. Wilson early noted that the evil never try to disprove the crimes in which they are caught; instead they smear the one who exposes them with a smokescreen to distract attention. Pilate, Caiaphas and any in danger of losing their positions always seek a scapegoat. An outrage on justice is perpetrated in a few moments and the burden thrown on the innocent. The persecutors never allow a fair hearing, for that would disclose that they have no case. By the time the public realizes this, the character assassination is completed and the reputation of the innocent ruined.

Persecution has been the lot of honest men in government. Because he exposed political thieves stealing millions, Richard Henry Lee is unknown to most Americans, although he had the greatest single day of any American when he introduced the Declaration of Independence, the Confederation and the alliance with France. For proclaiming liberty Samuel Adams was smeared as a "Communist" while James Otis was beaten by British officers till he lost his mind. Malice and hate followed Thomas Jefferson, the father of our country, and Andrew Jackson, the bringer of equality to the average man. William Jennings Bryan had three presidential elections stolen from him by small margins lest he bring in more opportunity and more democracy generations before they came. The haters of Franklin Delano Roosevelt agreed with his blunders but hated him for practicing Christian democracy. Harry Truman's devotion to justice for all earned him the genuine hatred of those who did not mind his mistakes. Estes Kefauver has no memorials because he exposed gangsters. Hubert Humphrey has been permanently persecuted because he has given his life to the American purpose of liberty and justice for all.

Conrad Noel was an English rector who devoted his life to liberty, one of the persecuted saints of our age. When he died, his bishop, Henry A. Wilson, a large-hearted evangelical, paid him one of the finest tributes paid to a man of our day:

> We are bidding a last farewell to a man who was the greatest personality in this diocese. His loss is irreplaceable. He was unique. He was in a class by himself. Little people may argue and dispute regarding his political opinions, but to me he was distinctive. He was never afraid to say what he thought and to fight for his principles; that is always a sign of a great man. He always displayed a rare courage, he never sought popular applause, and he feared only one thing: the shame of being untrue to himself and his convictions.
>
> I remember him giving an address on the political principles which were dear to his heart. I remember the fire in his eye, the flash, the zeal, the passionate enthusiasm of his words as he advocated those principles which, in those days, meant extinction of every hope of professional success, but such a thing as professional success never crossed his mind. Man must be true to himself or he is not man at all.
>
> I believe it to be literally true that he was the greatest personality among the clergy in this diocese as a student, as a writer, as a religious and political leader, as a man of artistic and musical sense, and most of all, as a saint of God. In him were assembled many and diverse gifts, any one of which would have given him distinction. His courage, which was unbounded, remained to the end, and as he lived so he died, a brave and faithful servant of Jesus Christ. Thank God for such men, and thank God it has been our privilege to meet one such through our journey through life.

SEVEN WORDS FOR TODAY

"Father, forgive them for they know not what they do." This is the biography of every man. We know not what we do. Even the most evil do not realize the awful consequences of their crimes and sins. None of those who crucified knew how evil a deed they were doing: not the soldiers taking orders, not the centurion giving criminal orders, not the cowardly governor letting an innocent man die to keep his job, not the thoughtless mob, not even the high priest who would lose $2 million graft a year if the temple stayed cleansed. Those who begin wars do not realize they may be destroyed by them. Those who start riots do not realize they may end as victims. Those who fail to stand against evil do not realize that it may end by ruining them. A mayor who refused to enforce a law against hogs in residential areas saw his daughter die the next month from a disease contracted from the hogs.

Our indifference is often more cruel than our wrongdoing. As Studdert Kennedy wrote:

> When Jesus came to Golgotha, they hanged Him on a tree;
> They drove great nails through hands and feet and made
> a Calvary;
> They crowned Him with a crown of thorns, red were His
> wounds and deep;
> For those were crude and cruel days and human life was
> cheap.
>
> When Jesus came to Birmingham, they only passed Him by;
> They did not hurt a hair of Him, they only let Him die;
> For men had grown more tender and they would not give
> Him pain;
> They only passed Him in the street and left Him in the rain.
>
> Still Jesus cried, "Forgive them, for they know not what
> they do";
> And still it rained the wintry rain that drenched Him
> through and through;
> The crowds went home and left the street without a soul
> to see;
> And Jesus leaned against a wall and cried for Calvary.

Three crosses shadowed the Judean sky as the world again crucified its Savior with its criminals. The world lives on a low level, but it punishes the criminal who lives on an even lower level. It also crucifies the good who live above the world. The world refuses to see the great gap between those who live above it and those who live below it, between the peacemaker and the coward, between the reformer and the destroyer, between the one who criticizes because he loves his country and his church and wants to make them better and the one who criticizes them because they are too good for him now. The other men were political criminals who had committed murder in the underground movement against Rome. One had the vision to see his Neighbor as the Lord of glory. "Today shalt thou be with Me in Paradise."

"Woman, behold thy son." The children of Joseph by his first wife would not care for Mary, so Jesus entrusted the care of the Blessed Virgin to his cousin and faithful disciple. God wants us to remember the mother who loves us and to remember all mothers and to make their lives better. We are members of the family of God. And all God's children have wings. Insulated and isolated from reality, modern man is exposed to so much tragedy day by day that he finds it hard to realize the deeps of sorrow. He must learn to live with all the children of God.

After speaking to his enemies, his companions on the cross, and all his faithful friends, Jesus mentions His own suffering, "I thirst." Like all these words, this widens and deepens with the years. We must remember He is God but we must also remember He is man. He was thirsty, hungry, sleepy as a man. All of God which could be contained in human life is Jesus, as the bay is the genuine salt water of the deep ocean. The thirst of Jesus was for men to live lives of character, for justice, for peace, for truth.

Everyone who tries to do right and who works for justice has the moment when he feels forsaken. For most run back when the going gets rough, most give up when the water gets deep. Jesus is almost forsaken on the cross by man and it seems God also has forsaken. But Jesus is quoting the first verse of Psalm 22, which begins with the feeling of being forsaken by God but works through to the triumphant conclusion that God is on His side. One of the startling evidences of the truth of the Bible is that centuries before David could portray the suffering on the cross and that Roman soldiers who knew no Hebrew and no Psalm said the words he foretold they would say. The cross is the price; the cross is also the victory.

"It is finished" was a cry of triumph. Finished was the suffering of the hours on the cross. Finished was the life of love like none the world has ever seen. Finished was the atonement, the reconciliation, the Lamb slain from the foundation of the world, the Suffering Servant who bore our sins and by Whom we are made whole. Finished was God's eternal purpose for the redemption of man. Only unfinished is our carrying to all men the good news that God loves men enough to die for them.

Jesus quotes again from the Psalms for His final word from the cross: "Father, into Thy hands I commit my spirit." The Christian can commit himself into no other hands than those of the loving Father. We entrust all who are dear to us to His never failing love, in death and in life. We walk the way of the cross which leads home. As the shadows lengthen and the evening falls, we come home to our Father.

LIFE, LIKE A PRISM OF MANY-COLORED GLASS, BREAKS THE WHITE RADIANCE OF ETERNITY

The One remains, the many change and pass;
Heaven's light forever shines, Earth's shadows fly;
Life, like a prism of many-colored glass,
Breaks the white radiance of eternity.

That Light Whose smile enkindles the universe
That Beauty in Which all things work and move,
That sustaining Love burns brightly.

God must mean very much what He is trying to tell us in color, for He placed it everywhere.

The windows of the new Coventry Cathedral in England are a series of colors symbolizing the changing scenes of life. This cathedral has been built anew, with special chapels for working

40

people, for students, for unity of all Christians. It has unusual architectural features along with traditional. But the major glory of the new Coventry Cathedral is the windows of color, especially the one which shades the colors of life into each other to show the changing years and the series on opposite walls which convey the same colors of life.

Life is a series of colors and this is symbolized by the gems of the New Jerusalem, described in the next to the last chapter of the Bible. The great Australian preacher, F. W. Boreham, was impressed by these stones when he read *Hitherto,* a Victorian story by Mrs. A. D. Whitney. My mother was impressed by the colors of the gems of the New Jerusalem from reading the same book as a young girl.

The Coventry Cathedral windows begin with the green which is the accepted color of youth. The stones of the New Jerusalem include the bright green of chrysolite and the deep green of emerald. It is a compliment to be called green; it means you are young, growing, full of life. God surrounds us with a world of green, especially in springtime, but not only then. He has set a restful background of green to much of the earth. The years of youth bring green days, full of hope and vision.

Next in the great window of colors, and in the side line of colors in the cathedral, is red, symbolized in the heavenly home by the sardius, our ruby, and the jasper. When red blood flows through the veins, when one is grown or imagines he is, when young manhood and young womanhood are pulsing with energy and strength, these are the red years of life. It is so important that then we paint in the galleries of memory pictures worth remembering, that we fit the mind with furniture mental and spiritual which will accompany us all our days. The service and sacrifice symbolized by this red remind us of suffering and love, and of the One who sat upon a throne like unto sardius and jasper together, Suffering Love Himself.

The middle panels in these windows are not of one color but are mixed, as are the middle years of life. The blue and the gray are in the windows and in the new Jerusalem. Many of our days are blue, and we use blue as an expression of sadness and dejection. But there are varied shades of blue, and the blue of the heavenly city is the bright blue of the sapphire. Durward Matherly, one of the best preachers I have known, and the best hospital chaplain, had a ministry of bulletin boards, changing the messages every day. A nurse of another church told him these messages had been her major inspiration, especially, "If you must be blue, for Heaven's sake, let it be bright blue." God has made the heavens bright blue and He wishes us to make the blue of our life bright blue.

Gray also marks the middle years, symbolized in Revelation 21 by the chalcedony, where gray predominates with stripes or streaks of white. We all know gray days, days like the traditional November of no color and no glow, drab and desultory. But Chesterton reminds us that events show up better on gray days, that gold shines better on a gray canvass. The gray of days is only part of the pattern and can be a background for brightness.

The windows have not only blue and gray for the middle years but also a green and a red. So does the list of precious stones in the Beloved Community. The green is not the green of youth, but the blue green of the beryl. There is still opportunity for some newness, some growth, some fresh beginnings. The red is the reddish brown of the sardonyx. The colors of autumn are deeper. This is not the red of young manhood, but it has still energy to climb high hills, to battle along the plateaus of life, to attempt and accomplish great tasks for God.

Coming closer to the center of one window and down the wall on the others we find the purple and violet of the senior years of life. The purple of jacinth and the violet of amethyst mark the foundations of the city of gold. For some the later years resolve themselves into the tragedy of the deep purple of jacinth, for others they become the violet twilight of amethyst. Life grows milder and mellower for many, and for all the shadow of nearby night sends its gentle haze over the twilight years. Yet here there is still the beauty of color and the wonder of splendor of the sunset.

The center and finale of the windows is gold, and the heavenly seer pictured heaven as a city of gold. The gold of topaz and of chrysoprasus completes the colors of the wall. Gold is the most brilliant, most precious and most splendid symbol the poet could use. The golden hues of heaven are beyond our earthly gold. Even our gold, when spun out finely, is clear as crystal. "Eye hath not seen nor the ear heard nor hath it entered into the heart of man, what good things God hath prepared for them that love Him." Our ears only hear a small portion of the harmonies of earth; our eyes only see the small interval of color between infrared and ultraviolet. The Lover of beauty who has made the snowflakes and the butterfly wings in delicate and varied patterns has new horizons of beauty for us beyond. From the rainbow in the sky at the beginning of the Bible story to this solid rainbow at the end, life, like a many-colored prism, breaks up the white radiance of eternity into the changing color sequences of life.

Mrs. Whitney has written:

> We should build a low, poor wall, of one stone perhaps. From the crimson of suffering we climb into the blue of truth and calm. White glistening chalcedony for purity, next flashed out the green, the hope of glory, then they mingle and alternate, the tenderness, the pain and the purifying; the veiled sardonyx stands for that, the life story. The blood-red sardius is the whole triumphant love which contains and overwhelms all suffering, the central and supreme type, crowning the human, underlying the heavenly. Then the tints grow clearer and spiritual; chrysolite, golden-green, touched with a glory manifest; the blending of a rarer and serener blue, the wonderful sea-pure beryl; then the sun-filled rapture of the topaz, and chrysoprase, where flame and azure find each other, the joy of the Lord and the peace that passes understanding. In the end, the jacinth purple and pure amethyst, into which the rainbow refines itself at last, hinting at the distance of ineffable things. The rainbow was a sublime sentence written on the cloud to stand forever. This rainbow of color is the eternal city.

Life, like a prism of many-colored glass,
Breaks the white radiance of eternity.

WHY SOUTHERN BAPTISTS GROW

Why have Southern Baptists in one generation gained six million members, more than there are in any other American church except two? Why have they grown more rapidly than any major church? Why do more Baptists worship every Sunday in our country than any other group? How have they managed to enlist over a million tithers and every day for a decade to turn a part-time church into a fulltime?

Baptists thrive in the geographical section and economic status with higher birth rates. Almost one-half of American children are born in the South and most babies are born in Baptist or Catholic families. Country people transplanted to town or city bring their rural religious allegiance, which is more Baptist than anything else. Baptists have gained in towns all over the South by continual recruiting of rural Baptists moved to town. The movement North and West of millions of Southerners has made Southern Baptists a national church almost unconsciously.

Millions of Southern Baptists attend each Sunday the Sunday School, morning worship, Training Union and evening worship. Who else can get out members four times a Sunday? Their lives center around the church and the doors are open almost every night for some organization or study class. Enthusiastic singing builds up fellowship. Young people grow up with their major fellowship in the church. For many in cities the church offers the individual the only contact where he is somebody.

The Baptist laymen do the work of the church and do not leave it to the pastor. Laymen often organize churches and they continually are on the lookout for new members. In half an hour at a Baptist Training Union you may have the experience I had in Nashville, of being invited to take part in the program, to lead the next program, to join the Bible class, to attend the Sunday School picnic and the men's fish fry and to move my letter. It would take years for this at many churches of other varieties.

Friendliness is a mark of a Southern Baptist congregation. If a boy or girl wants to get acquainted in a new place with others of character, the best place to go is the Baptist church.

In many cities in the South more young people are at Sunday night services in Baptist churches than in the movies and nightclubs of the town. While some churches afford only recreation to youth and thereby fail to hold them, Baptists offer training in Bible study, doctrine, worship and Christian living.

The local independence which has characterized Southern Baptists has made it possible to have different attitudes among churches of the same allegiance. This saves them from raiding by more emotional sects by channeling those with this preference into another Baptist church. It also makes possible historic worship in other churches. The continuation of Sunday night services is a mark of a living church.

Southern Baptists are intrinsically missionary. They have an urge to share the good news they have found and the faith and fellowship. They personalize missions and most Baptists know some of the thousands of missionaries they have. No Baptist church is devoid of many missionary-minded members. The same message and presentation which appeals to millions in America also appeals to millions in other lands. Every summer thousands of Southern Baptist students take jobs for their vacation where they can help start new churches.

Many on the outside have been unaware of the growing social consciousness among Southern Baptists. They had the only leadership in social concern who denounced the hatemongering of 1948. They opened their seminaries to all before some allegedly more tolerant denominations. They have taken seriously the education of black ministers. In many areas leadership against the saloon has been taken over by Baptists. The aggressive Southern Baptist press has more circulation in some states than the leading daily newspaper.

A major cause for Southern Baptist growth has been Biblical emphasis. The Bible is the basis of their sermons. Their simple doctrines have a profound appeal to the American mind and are in terms the humblest can understand. It is not a theology or a patristic creed but rather a collection of points on which in the process of time Baptists have found themselves united. Any attempt to extend it even to the Calvinism which

45

was once the prevailing mode of Baptist thought would prove inacceptable.

The preaching of the fundamental doctrines of the Christian faith is the strength of the Baptist message. Many who may not agree with all niceties of Baptist interpretation are attracted by the preaching of redemption and forgiveness. The modernist interpretation of a generation ago lost by default and liberal interpretations have been too diluted to stand in a world of conflict and fear. Institutionalists have survived, but with little attraction to the present generation. The people of this land, not only of the South, and not only of this land, are still hungry for the faith of their fathers, the gospel of the God who died for them on Calvary. Southern Baptists would be the last to claim that they have a monopoly on this, but the tired worker and the stumbling sinner who is each of us is always at home wherever he hears of the mercy of God and the love of Jesus.

UNTIL ALL THE FLOCKS ARE GATHERED TOGETHER

St. Bartholomew's Day comes when the urban church is apt to be at its lowest ebb of the year, in the last of August. Religion is at its height at this period in Southern rural sections, where, "If you can't get religion in August, you can't get it." But this is in nonliturgical revivals whose attendants have never heard of St. Bartholomew. A scant handful will greet the minister who holds service on this day. In the popular mind, the only connection that will occur is that some will recall out of dim pages in history that there was a massacre of Protestants on this day and therefore it is a time to refurbish ancient hates.

Paul Couturier, the French abbé who was ecumenical almost before there was such a word, had a brilliant inspiration as to the use of this day. He made it into a day of remembrance, but a day of contrition as well. He celebrated on St. Bartholomew's Day a mass of reparation, asking God's forgiveness for the massacre and for all the other evils committed by his church against the Huguenots. The next year other priests joined in similar services, and a historic occasion of animosity became a day for asking forgiveness of God for the sins of one's own church. It has been much more customary in gatherings considering unity to repent of the sins of others; this made it more personal and more real. To ask forgiveness of God and of man for the sins of the church in the past not only admits the church has sinned but suggests it may still be sinning. The third year some Huguenot pastors held services on the day confessing the sins of the past in murderous battles against Catholics and asking forgiveness for their part in the tragic wars of religion whose legacy is a France not even nominally Christian. The service spread and there is no computing how many services in France and beyond will be held this year to ask forgiveness for the part each church has had in rending the seamless robe and ill-treating fellow Christians.

Paul Couturier was a seemingly average priest occupied largely in teaching mathematics and science in a school for boys and in the parochial ministry attached thereto. He was two-thirds through his ministry before he felt the call to become an apostle of unity. By unity he did not mean submission of one church to another, and he deplored proselytizing. Unity was to come when and as God wills.

The Abbé Couturier was zealous in promoting unity by ways which may turn out to be more efficacious than large gatherings. He began a week of prayer for unity in January which by now is widely celebrated. He was certain that the primary path to unity was the path of prayer and that at moments when all other paths seemed blocked, this path was open.

The good abbé did not assume that faith without works would solve the problem. He felt that there could be no approach toward unity without a full understanding of other communions, of their faith and their works. In conferences and periodicals he strove to obtain and circulate free expressions of divergences and differences on major points. Unprecedented was a full issue of a missionary magazine by his Catholic friends telling of the

47

wonderful work of Protestant missions, and another devoted to Orthodox missions.

Could not Protestants take a leaf from Couturier's book and each denomination give one issue of its missionary magazine to narrate the great mission work of the Roman Church? And of other Protestant churches? Could we not give one article a month in our missionary magazines to a noteworthy work being carried on by others? What chance has the average reader of the periodicals of any church to know of the glowing splendor of the missionary labors of others? How can we even move toward unity when we do not know where others are and what they are accomplishing?

Could we not profitably spend the day set apart to the memory of a saint of whom practically nothing is known to consider some of our own shortcomings and sins which are not hidden from the chroniclers of history? The state church of England could ask forgiveness of the free churches for its persecution of them, and state churches of Lutheran persuasion could confess how far they went astray in their punishment of Anabaptists. The Church of Canada could contemplate its pressure against dissenting minorities, and the churches of South Africa could consider their sins of the past toward others. New England Congregationalists could pray for pardon for their treatment of Quakers, and Friends could ask forgiveness for the Scots on the frontier whom they refused to protect. Virginia Anglicans could consider whether their failure 360 years after Jamestown to number more than a fraction of the Baptists and Methodists in that state is not due to their reluctance to admit tyranny before 1776 and superciliousness since?

We could thank God for Vatican II and that the Roman Catholic church is drastically pruning pomp and ceremony, decentralizing authority and adding Bible study and Sunday night services, though many Protestant churches are going in reverse. We could thank the Methodists and Baptists for giving the gospel to Americans. We all might repent for our superior sneers at Pentecostalists.

We all need to confess the ways we have diluted the water of life and to pray pardon for the one-sided and warped personalities we have developed through our sinful sectarianism. We have produced Christians characterized almost exclusively by emphasis on doctrine, and others almost entirely emotional; some who live only by public worship and others by individualistic devotion. We have sects of shouting and of silence, of evangelism and of quietism. We do not develop all-round Christians even by our best emphases, unbalanced by opposite virtues. We all have something to contribute, but only as we come together. As was said in the first book of the Bible, "We can not until all the flocks are gathered together and the stone is rolled off from the mouth of the well."

THREE MODEST PROPOSALS

The scene was not clear. Although located in a wilderness, a cloudy haze made it seem at times the edge of a prosperous suburb. A conversation seemed to be going on between two very different persons. One of the two gave an impression of something not easily defined, but certainly which in the language of the time would have been described as supernatural, if not God-like. Although the outward appearance of the other seemed to fit in with a religious atmosphere, there was an indefinable something sinister about the man who seemed to have just dropped from a helicopter without bothering to change from his urban evening dress. He was obviously making some sort of a proposition to the man with the keen eyes of vision and the clear countenance of courage. It was evident that his first proffer had been rebuffed.

"But," insisted the gentleman in the full dress suit, "you are too intelligent to take my offer literally. You turn the material realities of life into spiritual truths. You can make the man who is poor and inclined to revolution into a guardian of the status quo by diverting his attention from such material complaints. You can make it clear that your gospel is primarily a way to making more shekels. Possession of your principles will gain money in the market place. It will enable men to sell more and to profit more, and who profits most, he serves best. Mammon can be transformed from a harsh stony word into a means of stewardship. Materialism can become a sacrament for the spiritual, so that whoever gains the most materially will be the finest man spiritually. This way you can even save millionaires, an unlikely happening under your preconceived theories. They will circulate your good news in little booklets by the million, and the isles of the sea shall rejoice—you see I have read Isaiah also. You will be invited to speak at conventions of dollar devotees as well as more to prosperous thieves. And who needs your message more? Are you going to deprive yourself of this opportunity to do good unto the most of these your brethren because of a few outmoded proof texts? Moses used manna and Elijah used oil; who are you to refuse to give this peace of mind to those who will thereby reward you handsomely, as well as becoming open to the rest of your teaching?"

But the answer was "Man shall not live by bread alone, but by every word that proceedeth out of the mouth of God."

The gentleman in the full dress suit suddenly disappeared. Or did he? It seemed as though he suddenly changed into a man with a clerical collar. It was doubtless an illusion; the two could not have been the same. They were dressed differently; they had widely distinct accents; and their propositions were not the same. But yet the observer thought he detected the same sinister atmosphere about the one who was making the proposition, while the radiance of the other seemed to glisten against the stone and sand of the barren hillside.

"My dear young friend," oilily insinuated the man with the clerical collar, "We have to adapt our message to the environment of the new age. Doubtless your methods would have worked in some primitive time, but they are obviously not suited for modern culture. This age is bored with listening and with looking. It takes something spectacular to attract interest. After they have seen the gimmick, then you can sell your story. That is the only approved technique we use today in mass communication. And we mean no reflection on the masses, for the elite and the Rotarians swallow their information by the same attention-getting routes as does the proletariat. Of course, we are not taking seriously those figures of speech about jumping off the temple. Unless it were carefully filmed—and there are limits to television, you know—it might just look ridiculous. Besides, so many people have jumped in movies and television and picture magazines that the stuff is old hat by now. What you need is a publicity department. No message can get far without it.

"We can get you a couple of good advertising agents. They will make your name a household word. People who have never heard of Caesar's first name or Herod's last will know yours. It can be done as easily as selling soap powder—and with infinitely better results. For once they are sold on you, you can lead them into this kingdom of heaven without any difficulty. Breaking then the sales resistance is the only problem. With your personality, it will be easy. You will have to restrain your adjectives about some of our leading citizens while we form them into a committee to preview your performance and to give the cash guarantees so necessary for mass evangelism. And you will have to adapt your message to the localities; you can't sell salt in Salt Lake City, nor can you preach against murder in Dallas nor against race prejudice in Detroit—I mean Nazareth. You will have to cultivate the local clergy; and nothing impresses them like big names, big headlines. We can get some free movies and some choice television time, if you will just cooperate.

"You will have to have a sponsor—no, not the crass commercial kind, with blatant bleatings of the product—just the mature institutional kind which mentions in a footnote in the local paper who was chairman of your local committee and what he sells. We have international connections: we can make you known all over the world. Don't think there are not chambers of commerce in other lands. We will provide the thousands to hear you. It's a simple trick. There are thousands hungering for sensations and thousands more hungering for a true gospel. If you don't fill that vacuum, some holyroller will.

"Think that over; is it better to let some splinter sect exploit this possibility because of your naive reluctance to use the tools of the trade? You will make millions, and of course you will not use them all for yourself. After providing for your family, your retirement years, your trips abroad for the recreation you

51

will need, your golf, and your well-publicized charities, you will have millions to give away. And it is more easy to advertise giving than receiving, and so we shall smother the criticism of the envious about what you make. By tying yourself in with Nero you will share his publicity.

"You will not even have to write your own sermons: we will have them airmailed to you a day ahead of time and written by the finest evangelists of the day. Your voice by microphone will stir the waiting throngs and by radio will go to the ends of the earth—and are you thinking of relying on the inadequate vocal equipment with which the Creator endowed us? You will have more converts than any man in history."

The voice persisted in quoting from possibly unhistoric contexts: "It is written, Thou shall not tempt the Lord thy God."

And once again the scene changed suddenly, as though in some new stage technique in which the hand is quicker than the eye, and the onlooker was not sure if this was a third personage making a proposition, or just the same actor in a different garb. But how could this be when his dress, his smile, his self-confidence, his air of realistic understanding seemed so far above the ones who had preceded him on this mount of what some might call temptation?

"I am glad you have not succumbed to the stupid and trivial propositions of my two predecessors," boomed the cheerful voice of the man attired in that sartorial resplendence of a senator, coupled with the sombre dignity of an undertaker. "I knew you were too smart for them; I told them so. They have assumed you were mercenary. They thought you were shortsighted enough not to see that their suggestions were only tricks of the adversary. They did not think you could see through their transparent temptations.

"Now, I offer you no temptations. I understand you. Only a brave and truthful gospel can be lasting good news. I will show you how to accomplish this. You do not have to take any suggestions from me. Just make it clear that you recognize the primacy of the practical. You are in this world, and you can use your own ways of fighting it. Just remember that pride is the key to ultimate victory in this sort of a world. Keep that faith in pride and power and you can evangelize the world in this generation.

"I am not proposing any trick stunts or any hocuspocus of materialism disguised as peace of mentality. I want you to be yourself. Be humble, and modest. Your way will be arranged for you. Your different accent will stand you in good stead. A Galilean voice is always interesting to flatspoken Judeans. You will not need a college education; we can find a seminary for you to attend long enough to mention you went there, but without any pride of education. It will show you are a self-made man not to have a degree. You will naturally begin with a village synagogue. While here, keep up your contacts with a city synagogue. When you get to a city, keep your eye on a capital synagogue. You are not seeking advancement, just a larger field for service. Some old man will be retiring from one of our greater synagogues by that time and you will naturally be his successor.

"Of course, you would not be that if you ever took embarrassing stands on social problems but after all it is your duty to preach against sin and heresy, and that will leave you no time for lesser matters of the law. You need not study, as you can use the sermons of others; after all, very few have heard them and fewer still have read them. In that city synagogue you will have members of the Sanhedrin. A few words modestly dropped about the spiritual possibilities of the chaplaincy of the Sanhedrin and you will have arrived. There you can pray and be reported by the media and sightseers will throng to your doors each Sabbath. You will naturally have a good press, with Sanhedrin officials in your congregation, and you will be a worldwide celebrity. Then you can preach the truth. This is no temptation —just a door of opportunity opening for your ministry."

The answer was somewhat shocking to the gentle pleader who had attuned his voice to friendliest encouragement: "Get thee hence, Satan. Thou shalt worship the Lord God and Him only shalt thou serve."

HERE COMES THE DREAMER

Genesis 38:19

Here comes the dreamer. He's just finished seminary. He is full of dreams of some great ministry, of opening the eyes of the blind and proclaiming the acceptable year of the Lord. He'll learn different. Wait till we get through with him. We are the stewards, the deacons, the vestry. We pay the money and we'll call the tune. We've seen these young idealists before. Where would our business be if we followed them? They do not know that cash is all that matters. Here comes the dreamer; he will change his ways; or he won't stay here long.

Here comes the dreamer. He has studied creeds, and all the history of the past, and all the varied viewpoints of the present. We'll get that out of his mind in a hurry. Ours were made up a long long time ago, and we're not going to change. He'll either preach as we believe or else. We have the truth we want right here in this church. And we won't have it changed. Forget those dreams, if you intend to minister to us. We want the same old hackneyed phrases, the platitudes, the preaching against sin at a distance; but you be sure and use the proper words, and don't leave out a single doctrine grandpa settled. And if you don't fence heaven with our trademark, at least make it clear we have the box seats there. Our glorious heritage we love to hear; and we will hear it from you, or from another.

Here comes that dreamer. He thinks that he can change our way of worship. It's been this way so long. We've always sung the same old songs, gone through the same old rituals as our great-aunts did. Your ideas are your own and you may keep them; we're very tolerant people, you will find. But don't you try to rearrange the service, or you will think that all hell has broken loose. The last fellow who tried it left so fast we shipped his furniture on to him. You understand?

Here comes the dreamer. He intends to work as if he were the one who runs this church. His professors forget to tell him it is ours. This is the only plaything some of us have. We have no husbands or they pay us little mind; but they don't care

54

what we do with our church. You listen to our voice; those who have not listened have had bitter days and their wives more bitter hours. This church exists for us to be important. Our organizations are more to us than any words in any Testament. Don't tell us what or how we shall do anything; we're older than you, and we'll have our way. When we are on your side, it's not what you think; we're only fighting that smart sister who thinks she can stop you with us against her. Soon as we put her in her place, we'll change and then you'll wonder what you did to make us enemies. Nothing at all; did no one ever tell you the pastor is a pawn in women's feuding? Here comes the dreamer; if he stays asleep, he'll do all right in our church; but if he wakes, he better get his traveling shoes on quickly.

Here comes the dreamer. He has visions of making this community a garden, of helping working men and cheering the aged. We'll let him do a little of that, but he must get it straight; we denominational executives expect a balanced budget and more giving. We do not care what sermons he may preach, what ritual he prefers, what methods he uses; only if he expects to get along with us—and we executives in church hold the power of life and death over his future—he better carry out our programs. By the time he carries them all out, he won't have time to disturb stolid bankers with welfare, justice, and good will. He will rise as he fits our pattern. The dreamer thinks he comes to preach a gospel; he comes to keep our chainstore wheels all turning in the name of religion that never offends, a tranquilizing gospel of euphoria; we'll waste his youth until he settles down to dreamless budget-balancing and pallid sermons.

Here comes the dreamer. Throw him in the pit and let him starve. No, sell him as a slave, and let him rest within an exile's grave. No, hang him on a cross. Here comes the dreamer. We'll kill the dream again.

NOT YOURS, BUT YOU

II Corinthians 12:14

Love is not possessive but giving, a concern to make life better for another. The parable of the Good Samaritan makes it clear that everyone we meet on the highway of life is our neighbor for whom we must do all we can.

What becomes of all the sweet little girls? There are more than you imagine, for many are carefully camouflaged, misled by stupid styles into imitating males instead of complementing them. The hideous cult of ugliness and the attempt to break down differences is a conspiracy to enslave us. A man is looking for a girl who reminds him of his mother, the most wonderful person he has known. The girl who fails to be feminine in its finest meaning is missing her opportunity.

Little boys have winning ways but little girls look more heavenly. The valley of girlhood, like Sharon in the Bible, is surrounded by forested hills of emerging problems. Beauty is from within and can enrich all around with trust and hope. The valley of Sharon lay between the Philistines who tried to wreck faith and the Phoenicians who substituted lust for love. To revolt against the moral standards of a mother can keep a girl from the home of which she dreams and plans and hopes.

Women tend to be conservative because they know that babies and grownup babies called husbands are much the same. There are no atheists in maternity wards. Women tend to have harder lives and to take themselves more seriously, for they are primarily concerned with a home, a husband and children. Motherhood is the major element in their life, even if it means mothering a classroom, an office or an organization.

Many women have as major aims getting the attention of a man and getting ahead of another woman. The girl usually determines dating and marriage, though she condescends to male obtuseness by letting the egotist think he is the pursuer. Dating has deteriorated into a status symbol by which girls seek marriage and most boys do not. We do not treat girls fair when we send them to school with boys of their own age whom

56

they find wearisomely immature. This often results in contempt for childish males, adolescent exploitation and fragile marriages.

Girls have to consider future generations in their health and morals. If the human race depended on the health and morals of the male, it would have disappeared long ago. The girl has to maintain high standards or she will lose more. The urge to dominate another is evil. Petting may result in marrying someone with whom you have nothing else in common. True devotion depends on a higher devotion. As Richard Lovelace wrote centuries ago

> *I could not love thee, dear, so much,*
> *Loved I not honor more.*

Many marriages fail to be their best because the husband and wife fail to realize that they are different psychologically and look at things differently. Girls and boys grow up in mostly separate worlds and they tend to stay in them. A home is not at its best unless each shares the concerns of the other. Many wives let their husbands down by disinterest in his work and recreation, while many husbands fail to share concern for the home. Many husbands are better because of their wives' faith in them. A home can become a haven of peace and joy.

The home is where we first learn the meaning of love. Love for father and mother, son and daughter, brother and sister, aunt and uncle, wife and husband can carry over to friends and neighbors. Because women deal primarily with personal relationships they tend to personalize everything, which is not always wise. Because the home is the center of her living a woman may tend to live within the small circle of herself and her family, when she needs to enlarge the horizons of the heart.

Love for a mother-in-law, who should be called a mother in love, for the relationship results from love rather than from law, is a sign of deep understanding. She is part of your life and can enrich it. Ruth was led to the true faith and understanding of life by the mother in love to whom she was devoted.

Genuine love does not seek its own, it is not possessive. Enhancing the ego by using another human being for our purposes is not love, nor when parents drag little girls out of the gardens of childhood or stunt little boys in little leagues for parental pride. Love is not blind; only hate is blind; love sees within and beyond to the inner spirit. Most of us have known the love of a mother and a father more concerned for us than for themselves. Genuine love is shown by sacrificing for each other. It is not love to let children do what they think they want to do in their inexperience and ignorance. A loving parent requires the child to do right even if it results in resentment. Love is deeply genuine which is so concerned for the other that it wants him to marry the one who will be best for him. Saints are people the light shines through, messengers of God who make us better for having known them.

Francis Xavier wrote of this highest love

> *My God, I love Thee not because*
> *I hope for heaven thereby,*
> *Nor yet because who love Thee not,*
> *They must forever die.*
>
> *Not for the hope of gaining aught,*
> *Nor seeking a reward,*
> *But as Thyself hast loved me,*
> *O ever loving Lord.*

To save the life of the man who was loved by the girl Sidney Carton loved, Sidney took the place of the man on the guillotine. A destroyer captain saw a torpedo aimed at a transport and turned into the path to be blown up and save the lives of all on the transport. When a Coast Guard captain was told it was too dangerous to try to rescue men from a sinking ship, he declared, "We have to go out; we don't have to come back."

THE SCHOOL OF LIFE

The entrance to the school of life is to repent, to change your mind. To repent is to readjust your mind to reality and when you repent you are rewarded with the fellowship of those who really live. Unless you are willing to learn, you can not enter. A student once told me why he was angry, "You called me ignorant and I'm in the ninth grade." I explained that he was ignorant, that I was ignorant, that we all are ignorant, but that some of us know that we are ignorant. Unless you become as a little child, you are not ready to enter the school of life.

"Great minds discuss ideas, average minds discuss events, small minds discuss people." The textbook is not all of the instructional material but it is a guide. We have the greatest textbook for the school of life and it is open to all who will read it.

"Life is the one great schoolmaster who leads us all to Christ," wrote William Tyrrell. "Who is a Teacher like unto Him?" asked Job. God himself shall be our Teacher in the school of life. Education, like faith, is caught, not taught.

The students who studied under Jesus attended the greatest and most progressive school. People could tell its graduates. He had no formal classroom; He taught people where they were, and what they needed. He taught the past as a guide to the present. He had no examination but character, no test but action. He gave only two grades, well done or not done. The homework was to live His teaching, the graduation, to teach others. He prepared them for the here and now as well as for the future. The alien Samaritan was His lesson of love. Is the Galilean still too great for our small hearts?

Grades in school designate the quality of teaching, not the quantity. Those who grade quantitatively grade themselves as incapable of quality. There is a great difference between those who are failing, getting by, doing well or doing excellently. F is a real grade and many write it over their lives. The average person wants to get by, with minimum learning, minimum faith, minimum morality. "What is the least I can do to be saved?" is his question. Churches which delude that some easy magic word or form will take him to heaven without living a Christian life can count on many members.

The B student does well and does all he is assigned, but no more. An A student does more than he has to, goes beyond what is assigned. He knows what is excellent and he excels. He walks the second mile, gives the extra measure, accomplishes another task. God would like us all to be His A students, his saints.

Some fail to be promoted in school for lack of attendance, attention and study. Basic faith begins on the elementary level, when we accept Jesus as our Redeemer. When promoted from salvation to surrender, we give our lives entirely unto Him. When we attain the serenity of implicit trust, we have come up higher.

A final examination is not a surprise but a sample of what you know. The final test is if you understand, not if you have memorized. When Jesus came to picturing the final examination of life, he had only one test: "Inasmuch as you did it unto the least of these My brethren."

As William Temple insisted, "God is not concerned only with religion, or even primarily." He is concerned with all our life. We must give to the needy, visit the sick and imprisoned, go to those in homes for the handicapped. When you vote for a candidate who is not concerned with helping the underprivileged, you vote against Jesus.

"Son, now you have an A.B., you must learn the rest of the letters of the alphabet," said the father to his son at commencement. The parent understood that commencement is really a beginning. Commencement is a result of years of study and other work.

The power of an endless life is electricity, not lightning, a current, not a bolt. It is not an isolated event in history or in the calendar but a power which can be turned on every day. Faith is not just a moment of conversion, but a current to light all our days. It does not change the furniture of life but it shows us clearer what is in the room. Faith is not given only on a special day, like a diploma; it is given day by day to those who use it.

Every day is commencement day. The way to resurrection goes by the way of the cross, His cross and yours, but the road leads home. The faith that lights all our days lights the way to eternity.

But warm, sweet, tender, even yet
A present help is He,
And faith has still its Olivet
And love its Galilee.

The healing of His seamless dress
Is by our beds of pain;
We touch Him in life's throng and press
And we are whole again.

OPEN THE DOOR

A college can not be a Christian college unless it is first a genuine college, a center of learning and culture. To love God with our mind is the divine obligation to be intelligent. Have you been taught not only to locate a fact but also to understand and relate it? Have you been taught to be critically intelligent and yet to hold fast that which is good? Have you been taught the true, the good, the beautiful, the divinely ordered life? As Owen Meredith wrote

More brain, O Lord, more brain, or we shall mar
Utterly this fair garden we might win.

This is the oldest college in this state. What results do we have to show for a century in this section? How many of our graduates are educated enough to attend our symphony concerts, our music recitals, our scholarly lectures? How many good high schools are there in our section, how many libraries, how many readers of books of value? Is our area distinguished for intelligent voting, for music which appeals to the mind rather than the feet?

In some miscalled colleges, classes are yellowed propaganda notes of ignorant isolationism, outmoded Darwinism, obsolete theories and misinformation by teachers who refuse to revise their flyspecked notes and their rote examinations, who ignore the library, and who never let students think. Their only advice is to enlist in their courses, and backslapping cliques keep their useless courses required. Some colleges offer so little for the mind.

Over half a century ago John Jay Chapman noted

> American colleges are guilty of treason as destroyers of the mind. Business control means reading and writing abolished, the disappearance of the educated man. Higher education shows the ravages wrought by ignorant wealth. A true university will never rest upon the will of one man nor be run like a business.
>
> A college president ought to be able to read and write but he need not be able to, so long as he can raise money. College presidents have been autocrats and sycophants. By hiring only safe mediocrities the dean or department is safe against criticism by administrators.
>
> The average professor will look on an act of injustice done a brother professor with the same unconcern with which a rabbit watches other rabbits killed. It would cost the non-attacked rabbit his place to express sympathy, and he is poor and has children and hopes for advancement. The professor seems to think it requires silence and discretion rather than exposure of educational abuses. He is trampled on, his interests ignored, he is underpaid and overworked, he is of small social consequence, is kept at menial employment, works tickers invented by men who should have been making timetables and leisure to do good work is denied him.
>
> With dumb reticence the faculty watch things of the mind devaluated. Colleges have been run by men remote from scholarship. Men are influenced by a few important contacts with one or two superior minds. The whole future of civilization depends on what is read to children before they can read to themselves. The thinness of our culture handicaps any who seek an education. A person trained only in science or business has no real education, is cut off from the past and denied the ability to express spiritual things.
>
> Loyalty to the truth is a fine thing; loyalty to anything else is an attack on truth. The truly religious man is ready at any moment to cast in the whole of his life at the price of truth and leave the outcome to God.

Remember that you live in the most ignorant age in human history. Computer ignorance multiplies dangers. Never have so many spent so much time looking and so little learning. Never have people known less of what really happens. We know more of the moon and less of the earth, more of murder and less of kindness, more garbage and less truth. We know how to fly but not how to drive safely. And we do not even know that we do not know, with our cluttered highways, jammed stadia and empty libraries.

Our ignorance of our ignorance is such that we spend more money for education than any country in the world and get less for what we spend. No other nation puts up with professors who can not speak correctly or awards degrees to those who can not read or write. We are so ignorant that we waste more money than any other people spend. We are so ignorant of how to get along with each other that we get most of the divorces in the world and so ignorant how to get along with ourselves that we drink most of the whiskey. And we are so ignorant of the Word of the Lord that our country is falling apart.

What you don't know will hurt you, in this world and the next. Carlyle said that the greatest enemy of the devil is the thinking man, but reason's halls are never crowded; they were not for Paul at Corinth. The present generation of American youth is the most ignorant in history, for all others have learned from their elders or from books, while it has done neither. Everyone has less sense in adolescence and whoever says otherwise is trying to exploit. As Adlai Stevenson noted at a commencement, "You know all the words I do, but 30 years have filled them with meaning." An irate listener phoned the radio station to cut me off when I was speaking on "My people perish for lack of knowledge," but the alert announcer advised him, "Mister, go back and listen; he's talking for ignorant folks like you."

More students than ever are cheated out of a college education. Genuine colleges are few which open the doors of the mind and set fresh breezes of thought sweeping through the open doors. Education is quality, not quantity.

"The teaching of fools is foolishness" as Proverbs attests, and no one is too incompetent, alcoholic, feebleminded or mentally deranged for some college to hire. Presidents and deans

63

devoid of intelligence and character find dubious dullards and illiterate anarchists who depersonalize students to whom they are inferior in courses empty of meaning. The scum which can not think and will not work has stumbled on the lush educational opportunities for kickbacks, payoffs and wholesale stealing. Subfundamentalist factories of falsehood and fanaticism brainwash with pharisaical phrases to swindle students out of an education. Almost every stadium has a college attached where they play school and teach ball and tackle a player as they would not let anyone tackle a yearling. Any college can lie its way into accreditation and parents refuse to believe what their children tell of the rottenness and emptiness of colleges.

It is no wonder students are in revolt, but if youth really wants to be different, it should try being Christian. We have to talk back to the big shots, to little men in places too big for them. When a college president said a student would come back and spit on his grave, he was answered, "Oh, no; I wouldn't do that; I never did like to stand in line."

> *The old men said to the young men,*
> *"Who will fight to be free?"*
> *The young men said to the old men,*
> *"We."*
>
> *The old men said to the young men,*
> *"Now, you are through, you can go."*
> *The young men said to the old men,*
> *"No."*
>
> *The old men said to the young men,*
> *"What is there left to do?"*
> *The young men said to the old men,*
> *"You."*

"Uncompromisingly Christian" is written on our walls, but not on our living together. If God is more than classes, how dare we go a day without joining in worship? If God is first, how can we fail to recognize Him at meals?

Are students our first academic consideration? Let us never quench the high and holy enthusiasm of youth. Can a Christian grade on a curve which ignores human personality? Didn't Jesus teach that people have a higher value than symbols? Do we decide questions democratically in faculty meetings by the mind of Christ? We do not have to be among the colleges which cunningly ensure commencement speakers will be devoid of ideas, which sell honorary degrees, which take stolen money. How many would give to us if they knew how we operate? Jesus comes second to cash on many church college campuses.

Are our classes in the way of Jesus? Are they any different from classes in a college which does not profess faith? The facts are the same; do we have any more light with which to interpret them?

Why do we not teach the literature which inspires character? Why do we use histories which give more space to Mohammed than to Jesus? History could be taught as His story. Is music for the glory of God or the glory of music professors? We could add to our library volumes of intelligent faith and use those we have. Our publications, recreations, dormitories could be Christian.

All facts are not created equal and an assortment of unrelated facts is not a reasonable facsimile of an education. The door of knowledge has been opened to many to whom the door of wisdom remains closed, for wisdom demands absorbing books by the score, scanning a page by the hour. Wisdom is the understanding of human days and destinies. The price of wisdom includes the willingness to follow truth through open doors to open still other doors. "Behold, I have set before you an open door."

SOPATER OF BEREA

Acts 20:14

To the Greeks, Berea was the noble meeting place of the Macedonian Confederation. The Romans also saw it as a noble town and so designated it. When Paul came there for the first time, he observed that the people of Berea were more noble than those of larger Thessalonica. Berea was noble by its history, and by its environment.

We know the name of one of the Bereans of that period: Sopater, the son of Pyrrhus. He is the only one of the early disciples in Europe whose father's name we know, which suggests he had an honorable ancestry, and that his father had been outstanding even among people of generous character. In an environment which shaped his formative years, and which was in itself an education, the reading of the Old Testament occupied a major place. Bereans were people who did not swallow credulously every new idea or reject contemptuously all that was not of the past; instead, they searched daily the pages of their holy Book to see whether the new teachings accorded with it. It was from this environment that Sopater went forth as a disciple of Paul, sharing with him the return to the Christian joy of Philippi, the voyage across the blue Aegean, the fury of the senseless mob of Jerusalem. As a missionary in his own right, he disappears from the pages of the New Testament, but not from the eternal annals of God.

Bereans found in their holy book the story of the cross which was to redeem them and all men, and also the cross which each follower of the Messiah would have to bear. They discovered in it intimations of the life to come and of the Risen Lord who should be its demonstration. Doubtless the apostle brought before them, as before his next audience at Athens, the great truth that "God has made of one blood all nations of Men." The Greeks felt themselves superior to other men, and to make them realize that God has only one race, the human race, and only one family, in which all are His children, was as astonishing and revolutionary as is the same teaching in some parts of the world today.

There was a simplicity to life in Berea, away from the furor and racetracks of Thessalonica, away from the demagogues and bustling commerce of Athens. In the more spacious leisure of Berea, perhaps more was understood of the wisdom of Athens than in Athens itself. Knowledge came and wisdom lingered, and there was time to assess the new in the light of the old.

From their study of the inspired Word, the men of Berea

could not be anything but puritanical. Futile hours of folly were not worthy of people who were striving to lead noble lives. The quiet of study needed not the stadium with its games or the forum with its idlers or the use of what would drug the mind and dull the conscience. Their heroes of the Old Testament were strong and sturdy nonconformists who scorned the customs of vanity. If, as Emerson assures us, "To be a man is to be a nonconformist," Bereans were evidently men.

It was impossible for Bereans to study the ancient volume and not to feel the passion for social justice which courses through it. The hot indignation of Amos at the exploitation of the poor and at the insincere religion of Bethel called forth another demand that a flood of righteousness submerge robber barons and dispensers of hypocritical ceremonial. The demands of Micah echoed forth that men must learn to do justly and love mercy. The tremendous realism of the lonely prophet of Anathoth brought forth in others the infinite compassion which scorns selfish patriotism, narrow churchmanship, and a social order steeped in selfishness. Bereans could look with Zechariah for a society in which even the bells on the horses and pans in the kitchen should be part of a social life made holy to the Lord.

Berea was not to be unmolested in its innocence and faith. Neighboring bigots and stormtroopers of prejudice stalked in to disrupt the new-found harmony of life and truth. They did not destroy the faith of Berea, but they did disturb it. There are always those whose darkness must haste to shut out the light, lest they be seen for what they are, and their hates exposed to the sunlight of brotherhood. But the invasion of ignorance did not end the gospel in Berea, and its Bible-believing people continued to walk the more noble ways of living.

Berea was as a city set on a hill, an example to larger places not characterized by the same nobility of insight and outreach. Its church grew slowly in the unity of spirit and in the bond of peace. Those who had grown up in its environment were marked men. One could undoubtedly recognize them in the early centuries of the Christian era, men of calm and serene trust in the God of all men revealed in the love of Jesus.

But not all who lived in Berea had the Berea spirit. Geography does not necessarily persuade or environment convert; heredity fails in obvious instances, and faith is not irresistible to the hardhearted or softheaded. Nobility did not necessarily rub off on all comers. Those who came without the right spirit left without having absorbed it. The culture and faith of Berea rolled off them like the proverbial water off the duck's back. There were those who infiltrated the community with the desire to be known as noble, rather than to be noble, and to whom the Berea spirit was such a challenge to their own triviality that they sought to level it down to the essential mediocrity of every age.

We do not know all the history of Berea, save as it is the history of every place where men and women set themselves aside to follow the good and the true, and where youth is steeped in deep draughts of man's heritage of the eternal. Insofar as those were Berea, they stamped their imprint on many a generation, which went forth and whose purpose held to sail the distant seas, to strive, to seek, to find and never to yield. And the sunset of the seas flecked with blue and white carried them "To where beyond these voices there is peace."

IN HIS NAME SHALL THE GENTILES HOPE

Matthew 12:21

Pre-Freudian, pre-Marxian, pre-Einsteinian—these adjectives are appropriate for much which is said in criticism of Christ as the hope of the world today. Guilt complexes stimulated by the rigorous demands of the gospel, economic motivations interfered with by His teachings, dwellers in a fixed Newtonian universe which evaporated before Hiroshima are paralleled by churchmen who live mentally in a fixed 19th century world with staid Victorian furnishings, to whom the living Christ means the destruction of their comfortable status quo. They become apoplectic at a hope of Advent, because this word suggests that their social order is impermanent. The hope of Advent confounds those who have used the American Dream as a vehicle for their messianic complexes, and deranges the plans of those who have followed the tradition of court bishop Eusebius in expecting the heavenly city to set up its celestial housekeeping where "the beauty that was the wilderness and the spirit that was the pioneer have become the thingful emptiness of a Midwestern town."

Likewise anathema to the upholstered classes is the hope of hell, which keeps faith in eternal justice strong among millions who see no opportunity of freedom in their lives or of unfettered worship of the Christ who comes in glory. Hell has much more validity as a hope to a generation which has produced its own reasonable facsimiles of hell, and which is endeavoring to improve on its amateur attempts. The increasing sadistic cruelty to which even kindergarten readers of alleged comics are subject makes an eternal answer to cruelty vital. There has to be a hell for those who make this world a hell for others. Those who doubt such a contingency may merely be suffering from social guilt complexes, and their bitter resentment of any mention of hell is obviously a rather shallow rationalization.

Safe in their sinecures, pensions, or ecclesiastical WPA's, the veterans of the Fundamentalist-Modernist warfare of the 1920s are apt to think that this is the opportunity for them to renew that conflict on a more global scale; but they fail to realize that their concepts are as obsolete as a shiny A model of the '20s. The Institutionalists, whose primary concern is with the outward unity which balances budgets, maintains a solid front against competing sects, and grows in statistics—if not in grace —won the fight of the '20s. Few denominations let either their left or right wings get away from the fellowship of the exchequer. Theoretically, the Modernists won, because they managed to hold the positions from which the Fundamentalists attempted to oust them; but, in the long run, the non-ecclesiastical forces of biology and cultural patterns have given the victory to those who would have been labelled Fundamentalists years ago. The onrushing tides of Southern Baptists, Negro Baptists, Missouri Lutherans, and Pentecostal Assemblies of God have changed

69

the perspective of American religion; the churches with children, and therefore with the future, are not the liberal groups. This has also been evident in the recrudescence of sectarianism, in the increase of conservative institutions, and in the marked conservatism of ministerial candidates for decades. Wars and depressions have driven many to positions of the past which are not intellectually untenable. To an increasing number of Americans traditional eschatology is more meaningful than it was a generation ago, and Christ the hope of the world is a part of their sermonic diet every Sunday; in which they are one with the European theologians who name eschatology as central in the life and thought of the church. Is it just the comfortable churches of respectability who frantically protest that the doctrine of the second coming of Christ is intellectually disrespectable while at the same time they view the second coming of William McKinley as within the range of economic possibilities?

For Christ as the hope of the world is by no means the private property of the churches. The Gentiles also have a share in this hope. Ecclesiasticism is as suspect among many American working men as it is among restless Asiatics or awakening Africans. It is all too obviously evident that the gains for the common man in this generation did not come from the churches. Only indirectly have they even influenced the political and economic measures whereby the forgotten man has been enabled to live better. It is no secret that the decline of British churches was accompanied by a rise in faith in the British Labor Party as the institution in which the lowly put their trust. What centuries of churches state and free failed to bring have been brought into existence in a decade: better housing, schooling open to all, health cared for from the cradle to the grave, the opportunities of helping shape the destinies of the world, and of feeling themselves a real part of God's creation. Christ the hope of the world has come to Britain through the Gentiles.

There are devout churchmen in our land who would suffer from apoplexy if it were suggested to them that God's new Messiah for this age is to be found in a political party. It is obvious that every political party has, like any church, more than its quota of misfits, mediocrities, wardheelers, spellbinders, grafters, and neanderthals; but it remains true that more work of Christ has been accomplished in the social realm here through a political party.

Churches have pleaded for centuries for pitiful doles for the old; the old have received their first small measure of justice through the secular state. The cause of dependent children received tearful entreaties and small contributions from the churches before becoming a state responsibility to which none may dodge contributing. Churches have voted social creeds but it took senators to give the worker the rights of a free man. Church leadership fought against child labor for generations but it took politicians to end it. Rural religion was concerned with the plight of the small farmer but the farmer received his aid from Washington while some blighted areas blossomed like the rose from political measures. The more abundant life has been brought to millions through a political party whose members are mostly connected with theologically conservative churches and who regard Christ as the hope of the world in government as well as in church. The human rights whose denial the author of Lamentations declared that the Lord would not countenance, the standards of fairness which Ezekiel asserted the Eternal has ordained, the ultimate verdict of inasmuch on judgment day has been approached more by the people of God as a democratic government than as a church. How many churches are willing to implement locally these standards of government? Is it any wonder that devotion, enthusiasm and zeal exists in many lands for democratic parties as the hope of our generation? Is the Galilean still too great for small and sectarian souls, but not too great for political parties of democracy and brotherhood?

COOPERATING WITH THE INEVITABLE

"What you have in mind shall not be," noted Ezekiel (20: 32). The illusions, delusions and hallucinations that the future would be a continuation of the past of oppression and exploitation were rebuked by the prophet. An old Negro explained how he had managed to endure his hard life, "I learned long ago to cooperate with the inevitable."

It took the swirling waters of a Red Sea to make a pharaoh learn to cooperate with the inevitable of letting God's people go. It took almost complete destruction of the Benjaminite defenders of murder to bring Israel out of the shadow of states rights into the sunshine of human rights. It took the warnings of the town clerk to break up the states rights mass hysteria of Ephesian greed. Similar stupidities of failing to cooperate with the inevitable led to a scaffold in Whitehall, a rope on the green, a guillotine on the street, a cellar in Ekaterinburg, a fiery grave in Berlin. You do not have to give in to wrong but you do have to learn to work on the side of the forces that work for right. Life has no place for Rip Van Winkles and Canutes. The stars in their courses fight against exploitation. This is an inevitable with which we must learn to cooperate.

> *The guns that spoke at Lexington*
> *Knew not that God was planning then*
> *The trumpet word of Jefferson*
> *To bugle forth the rights of men.*
>
> *Had not defeat upon defeat,*
> *Disaster on disaster come,*
> *The slave's emancipated feet*
> *Had never marched behind the drum.*

Deluded were the rulers of Memphis whom Isaiah saw failing to comprehend the inevitable and instead looking outward, downward and backward. They spent more on clothes and cosmetics because they valued the body above the spirit. They made Memphis safe for chariots and safe from fire but not safe for democracy or safe for faith. The rulers of Memphis did not mind murder and crime but they hated being exposed. They looked down on a river as dirty as a river town of vice and degradation, down on the hungry and exploited toiling fellaheen. Million dollar sectarian temples gaudy with greed never challenged the power structure of arrogance and exploitation. They looked backward and blindly fought against every improvement till the city became covered by the shifting sands of the relentless desert.

God laughs at the tiny exploiters who have the hallucination that they are superior, at the arrogance of atheists who think they run the world, at the illusions of generals who ask worship, at imperialists who exploit others and nationalists who delude their own. The Eternal laughs at the racism masking inferiority, the Baalism testing all by the dollar sign, the sectarianism making God the private property of some sect, some ritual, some religious structure. They go the way of all which fails to cooperate with the inevitable.

We have to learn to cooperate with the inevitable of fighting the same battles over in every generation. Battles won by the preceding generation do not remain won. Gardens have to be replanted, fields reweeded, dishes washed again and again. The same tasks confront us as faced our forefathers. As Alice was told in Wonderland, "Here you have to keep running to stay where you are."

The Jubilee in Leviticus set up a permanent revolution to prevent poverty. The devil has an answer for every improvement. One-third of our people opposed liberty in 1776 and in 1968. The battle has to be fought anew in every generation for freedom to speak the truth, to publish the facts, to support unpopular causes, to be tried by due process rather than by headline and hearsay, to preach an uncompromising faith hated by the world order. Slavery and alcoholism recur in every generation from greed preying on ignorance. Insecurity ended in one generation returns in the next. Peace does not last without renewal. Increased literacy is counteracted by increased publication of trash not worth reading, to distort and misinform. Added leisure has been taken over by the idiot box and wreck-reation. Most can now attend college but a diploma is only evidence the graduate was not in the penitentiary on commencement day.

We have to learn to cooperate with the inevitable will of God. The will of God is a relentless river which nothing can halt. God's will shall be done, even if we try to block it. If we are

73

faithful, God has willed His truth to triumph through us. God wills that men shall live in brotherhood and they shall. Franz Werfel was booed off platforms by Nazis 40 years ago for pointing out the choice was not between Right and Left but between Above and Below. It still is.

> They are slaves who fear to speak
> For the fallen and the weak.
> They are slaves who will not choose
> Hatred, scoffing and abuse
> Rather than in silence shrink
> From the truth they needs must think.
> They are slaves who dare not be
> In the right with two or three.

The unpardonable sin is to be wrong in your basic moral judgment, to call good evil and evil good. There is no right to be wrong on the major issues of life. You may commit the unpardonable sin if you support a party or a candidate of hate. In 1928 I warned that religious hate crucified Christ anew. Hate blinds you, drives you insane. In 1948 I began a sermon, "Everyone who votes for the miscalled Staterights ticket is going to hell." After a pause, I corrected myself. "No, every one who votes for the Staterights ticket is not going to hell; he is in hell now, for he that hateth his brother is a murderer and no murderer has eternal life." In 1968 I had to warn again that anyone who lives in hate can not live in God.

Age happens to the best of us. So does death. "Poor little monk," sympathized a Saxon knight as he watched Luther confront the might of empire. The essential dignity of a brave little schoolgirl against the insolence of ignorance, the oppressed toiler deciding he would rather be in his grave than be a slave, the broken voice of blind Fanny Crosby singing "And I shall see Him face to face," these are evidences of cooperating with the eternity in our hearts. False faith may fall before a storm but real spring follows winter. What looked like rows of tombstones turned out to be lighted windows: a parable. The forgiveness of sins, the resurrection of the body and the life everlasting mark the height of reality in God in which our lives find their ultimate meaning.

God is the Eternal Radical. He goes deep down to the roots. His thoughts are not our thoughts nor His ways our ways. He puts down the mighty from their seats and exalts the humble and meek; He fills the hungry with good things and the rich He sends empty away. We see God the Eternal Radical acting through the pages of history, the rise and fall of empires, the destruction of the empires of the early part of this century, and in today's happenings.

God is the Eternal Liberal. He is the generous giver of every good thing. He gives us the scarlet hills of autumn and the symphonies of the spirit, opportunities and grace, poets and saints, men and women of good will. He is ever gracious to all, merciful and kind.

God is the Eternal Conservative. In Him all things cohere. The universe holds together through Him. The Eternal is our dwelling place and He establishes the works of our frail hands. The excellent becomes the permanent, for the only permanency is in Him. His purposes are beyond defeat. Augustine wrote, "Blessed is he who loves Thee and his friend in Thee and his enemy for Thee, for he alone loses nothing in Him who can not be lost."

God is the Eternal Dawn. He was the Dawn of the resurrection morning when as the first day began to dawn, they came to the tomb. He is the Dawn of every life, of every new purpose of hope. Dependable dawn assures us that the sun will rise: and so He brings us to the desired haven. May the dawn of this day dawn on you every day, the Eternal God, giving, forgiving, remaking, keeping, dawning. We face death with courage and confidence because the God who saved us here is waiting for us there. "And when the morning was now come; Jesus stood on the shore."

THE OLD IS BETTER

Luke 5:39

The old is not necessarily good, but it is apt to be better than the new, because it has been tried. A genuine conservative does not fail to empty his wastebasket daily nor does he save the garbage of yesterday. He knows to discard the hull and shell of the walnut to get the real meat and he knows how to discard the husk of the past without losing the grain. A conservative is not a reactionary who tries to put a butterfly back into the chrysalis nor does he light a fire under his car because it worked on the old mule. A thief is not entitled to be called a conservative because he wants to keep what he has stolen. A conservative does not keep both feet still but he knows better than to try to keep both in motion at once. Conservatism involves faith in classics which picture the essential attitudes in different circumstances, in culture which carries forward the growth of the past, in deep understanding of human days and destiny and of the tragic sense of life.

Human beings are much alike in all ages and conditions recur in a constant pattern. The best of the old world is here. European history is an immensely overpaid account and it is much more important to see across the Appalachians than across the Atlantic. The pioneer was a basic conservative who carried with his plow and his family his laughter and song, his Bible and his God, and he founded a new society on the old security. American conservatism includes the Puritanism which in Virginia as well as Massachusetts gave us a serious and intelligent outlook on life based on faith in God and resulting in free inquiry, free speech, free government, free enterprise, free ordered ways. The God who led the children of Israel across the sea that was red led our ancestors across the ocean that was blue.

Conservatism conserves its beginnings and ours include a revolution for the faith that all men are entitled to equal rights. We can not go back on the document which bugled forth the rights of men and claim to be conservatives. Any attack on the essential right to life and liberty is unAmerican.

Equal does not mean identical but protection for life and opportunity for education, housing and employment are part of our basic heritage. Liberty and justice are for all, including the neglected poor white, on whom the burden of desegregation has been laid. Civil rights are also for whites. There is no civil right to commit civil wrong. The trumpet is still blowing liberty throughout the land to all the inhabitants thereof.

The conservative knows that the general welfare requires helping those in need through a welfare program. Our welfare payments are made almost entirely to the old, blind, crippled, widows, children; less than 2 of 100 receiving these are men of working age and very few of them capable of holding a job. Yet those with guilty consciences for helping cause the poverty which makes such expenditures unavoidable continually yelp against all welfare.

We are all on welfare; you, too. We all receive money directly or indirectly from the government which we did not earn. The rich get more welfare than the poor; their tax deductions cost taxpayers 10 times as much. Highways are welfare for rich contractors and billionaire auto companies. The trillion dollars on defense is more costly welfare given to the 100 richest corporations. TV franchises are welfare given on the air which belongs to all of us. The press is subsidized by letter postage, as is much advertising. Railroads, planes, shipping have been given untold billions in welfare. Federal cash to rich farmers is more welfare than their tenants get in a lifetime. Government contracts keep many businesses going and millions on governmental payrolls in military or civil or college service are given much more welfare. The poor pay for the welfare of the rich and the middle class pays the income tax. Clergy should be the last to complain about welfare.

The American conservative believes in the constitution, not as a set of infallible prescriptions, but as a realistic understanding of men who understood original sin well enough to prevent anyone from having too much power. A constitution written today would be worse. The conservative believes that the people have the last word. He is opposed to letting Congress tie its own hands with senility and cowardly ineptitude, to presidents

77

dictating, to courts arrogating unwarranted authority to themselves. The conservative believes in the general welfare and the common defense, both of which were conservatively carried over from the older Confederation.

The conservative knows that officials are under authority and responsible to God and man. He knows the Bill of Rights is to protect us against them and against any other power which usurps the power of government. He knows civilians may be more bloodthirsty than soldiers and the State Department less peaceable than the Defense Department, but he knows liberty is lost when those whose power and profit depend on war have the final say. He knows our generals and Russian generals join in frightening us into spending more billions when no defense is possible against missiles destroying most of our people any moment, no defense but peace.

The genuine conservative knows that justice must be given to all, not just to those who can spend thousands of dollars for lawyers. He is depressed over the declining character of judges and over cowardly congressmen who refuse to overrule criminal courts. The conservative follows the Bible in knowing that life can not be preserved except by taking away legally the lives of those who destroy other lives. There is no right to life unless the one who takes life is kept from repeating his crime. Capital punishment by government is the only alternative to capital punishment by murderers. More murderers inflict capital punishment every year than government has inflicted in a century. Only one choice is possible between the lives of our children and the lives of murderers. Sloppy sentimentality aids those who wreck human life.

The conservative knows that murder of mind and soul is worse than murder of the body and he realizes that we must eliminate those who do worse than murder. God ordained a death penalty for sodomy and has never repealed it. Perversion is treason to the human race and will wreck any nation. Unless we eliminate those who are murdering body, mind and soul, they will kill us off, and they are doing so.

The conservative knows that destroying respect for women by flagrant obscenity and sadistic lust is to destroy America.

78

Mediterranean scum who pour their filth into children's eyes and minds are enemies of the American way of decency. The sinister sabotage of Sunday night is a denial of religious freedom to Protestants. We are a Protestant people entitled to our traditional day of rest and worship unmolested by purveyors of filth and greed. Emerson observed that free institutions would go if our Sundays were stolen from us. Those who did not grow up in Sunday School rarely comprehend American life.

The conservative realizes that class determines our attitudes and actions more than race or nationality. We are born into a certain class, and although we may rise from it, not many do. The only real high class consists of those who live on a higher level. This class is marked by social concern, personal responsibility, consideration, imagination, initiative, restraint, critical thinking, independence. It is at home with history and music, ideas and books, has a sense of humor and unconcern for money, style, conformity.

Essential is a middle class with seriousness, patriotism, a sense of law and order, respect for womanhood, taking church and school seriously. The home is the center of its living. Unfortunately every social order has a lower class, marked not by lack of money but by irresponsibility and anarchy, by doing what it wants to. Anti-intellectualism, resentment of intelligence, aversion to books and music, superstition and suspicion, inertia, servility, credulity characterize it. It lives by its feelings, succumbs to current crazes, resorts to violence, lacks respect for women and for property. Society has to be on the alert always to prevent these, most of whom are not poor, from destroying civilization.

The conservative realizes that the networks have refused to allow the truth of Jesus to be preached and that one network even eliminated sermons because they might awaken listeners to realities. Diluted presentations and outright counterfeits of the gospel have been broadcast for years, but not one continuous program which would bring listeners face to face with Jesus. Attacks on Christian faith and morals are made daily, but no answer is permitted. If the networks really allowed the millions of Americans who believe in Christian faith and morals to have

79

their message brought to all instead of the unbelief of a minority of a minority, people might learn that network values are opposite to those of Jesus and might prefer the truth as it is in Jesus.

Southerners have a fellowship of the conservative understanding of life, which is the opposite of what our scalawags bootleg. The person counts for more and is basic in our personal relationships which span other lines. We are easygoing and good-natured and because we know we will never be rich, life is not engraved with the dollar sign. "You all" is our symbol that you are part of your family and community in our social apprehension of living. To us Dixie is a song of love, not of hate, and the Stars and Bars a symbol of the South, not of race. We fought against Yankees, not against blacks, and more blacks served under it than under the other flag. Warmth, ease, accent, humor, British background makes us as different as Scotland is from England. We are basically Celtic in names, emotions, intuition.

Because we are of one background we have escaped the ethnic divisions of the North and we have less religious prejudice. Catholic candidates for president have found most Southern counties on their side, and only a few hundred other.

We are conservative Americans because we made the declaration and a constitution and have retained an allegiance to and understanding of them which has strengthened every major advance in American history.

We are realistic because we learned in a fellowship of suffering how little tragic wars and reconstructions accomplish. We have been through this before. We know the impossibility of winning all wars or solving all problems, and our realism stands more chance of surviving than shallower solutions. We note discrimination against Southerners is still legal.

Our government under God was brought over by Puritans from Britain and our tradition stems from Calvin and Augustine. The American Roman Catholic Church is the strongest Catholic church in the world, because Protestants made it freer. More Jews live in our land than in all the rest of the world put together because American Protestants gave liberty to the people of the older Testament. Protestantism made possible the opportunity to worship God in other ways. Every major movement in our history has had a religious motivation and even the Supreme Court has discovered that we are basically a religious people.

"Congress shall make no law to establish articles of faith or a mode of worship" was the first draft of our present First Amendment, and makes clear its meaning. It sets up no separation of church and state; it requires government to support religion. Chaplains in Congress and armed services, prayer in court, exemption from taxes, religious services in penal and charitable institutions are part of this freedom of religion. William Johnson of South Carolina, the first justice named by Jefferson, and the first great dissenter, gave the mind of the court in a decision which the recent court seems never to have read, and which sustained the requirement of faith in God.

> Requirement of belief in God is not a sectarian test; it is a test of sanity. The statute does not require belief in a Christian, Buddhist, Mohammedan God; it only requires belief in a Supreme Being. Anyone who does not believe in a Supreme Being above him to Whom he is responsible is not sane.

Our constitution is based on the written covenants of the Old Testament and its framers had no intention of authorizing atheism, which they regarded as treason. Gouverneur Morris, one of the less orthodox, expressed the mind of the framers when he insisted "But the most important of all lessons is the ruin of every state which rejects the precepts of religion." Freedom of the press does not include freedom to destroy the press, nor freedom of assembly freedom to destroy assembly.

The constitution does not allow attacks on faith in state-supported colleges or schools nor the requirement of reading books destructive of faith or morality. No one has the right to try to destroy basic morality or to teach what he knows is not true. Tax money may not be spent to destroy religion.

The elimination of religious services for students is unconstitutional. They are entitled to the same right to services as those in mental hospitals, prisons, armed services. No educational institution has the right to refuse to teach the major factor in history, the Christian faith, or to ignore the greatest Person in history. The college or school omitting the Bible is presenting a warped viewpoint and an unAmerican. Even the Supreme Court has pointed out that history and literature can not be correctly taught apart from the use of the Bible.

We hope for more devotion to our fathers' God Who made us a great people. It is to our fathers' God we appeal and under Whose judgment we stand. In Him we trust. This is the American faith.

SLIPPERY WHEN WET

"Slippery when wet." You are familiar with these warning signs. You drive more carefully, you stop to think when you realize that highways are slippery when wet. But wet roads are never more slippery and dangerous than false arguments to make you forget that, as Emile Leger, who gave up being Cardinal of Montreal to become a missionary to African lepers, insists: "90% of man's misery comes from alcohol."

Alcohol is no more a gift of God than a rattlesnake. God did not make everything to be swallowed nor is everything as it was before the fall. God no more made whiskey and fortified wine than He made poison gas or Nazi kilns. The abuse of the gifts of God is a sad part of human history. Yet a report made to a national church convention, though never adopted by it, used such infantile irrelevancy of argument and moronic mentality by describing as attractive the submergence of mind to emotion produced by drinking. It used the same pharisaic self-righteousness of those defenders of a less profitable slavery a century ago, which the same church also never opposed.

The naively adolescent report included the guilt complexes intrinsic in such pseudo-humble pharisaism but no sign of the compassion of the Carpenter of Nazareth. To conform to the present evil world may attract the stationwagon set who never take Jesus seriously but it is unlikely to appeal to those in need.

The organization man will welcome any ecclesiastical reinforcement of conformity and the flannel suit the flannel mouth. Suburbia is enthusiastic over anything that destroys thinking and obviously, this report is not intended to appeal to intellectuals. There is no suggestion that the time and money wasted on alcohol could be used for books, so scarce in Suburbia, and on thinking, also scarce. The author has not read Upton Sinclair's *Cup of Fury* and learned how many recent writers killed themselves with alcohol.

It is most remarkable that the writer seems not to have read Aristotle, the apostle of moderation, or his definition of moderation: "Moderation includes restraint in the use of harmless things and total abstinence from harmful things." Otherwise the golden mean becomes the yellow streak.

It also appears that he has not read T. H. Green, the great Oxford philosopher:

> As with ignorance, so with intemperance. The gin-shop is an external thing that is evil, and if intemperance is as much a hindrance and obstacle as ignorance, the state may ask its citizens to limit or even give up the not very precious liberty of buying and selling alcohol, in order that they may become more free to exercise the faculties and improve the talents which God has given them. It makes no difference that the state in education puts compulsion on the father for the sake of the son, and if the other puts compulsion on each and all for the sake of each and all.

The report floats in a vacuum, with total disregard for science which shows how every drink diminishes the mind, and for sociology, with its mass of data on the results of alcohol on society and social groups, and with no regard for criminology, which has enormous information on the correlation between drinking and crime. What respect for science can be expected from a church which still uses the contagious common communion cup? One would never guess from the report that an innocent sport like drinking was connected with the majority of serious crimes. Nor would one gather that most of the thousands murdered by automobiles are killed by drinking drivers.

Moderation here is even more dangerous, as you may recognize a drunken driver or he may go off the road before a wreck; it is the man who has had a few drinks and thinks he is just as good as before who kills other motorists. There is nothing in the report about the moderate drinker as a hazard to himself and to others on the way home, no evidence of knowing elementary facts as to how one drink reduces the margin of safety by making it take longer to reach for the brakes, to make a turn, to make a split-second decision.

There is also innocence of psychology and psychiatry. The report does not deal with the feebleminded, insane, neurotic, paranoic and schizophrenic urges which alcohol increases. The report would never, never, be so indecorous as to suggest that there might be something mentally or emotionally wrong with the man who craves even a moderate amount of alcohol. There is no suggestion that much drinking may result from inferiority complexes, from people who do not have good sense, and do not want to admit it. The frustrated who frustrate themselves further with alcohol are ignored.

The report betrays a total unconcern with government and law and its philosophy. It appears ignorant of the lawless institution the liquor traffic has been, from the time it bootlegged firewater to start Indians on the warpath to today when it furnishes the second largest revenue to gangsters and the underworld of crime and murder. One would never guess from the report that police look in saloons when they are hunting criminals, or that night clubs are a major source of income for racketeers. There is no mention of bribery by drinking in business, or of drunken commanders who have caused thousands of casualties. The Pentagon would lose less battles if it did not train officers to drink. There is nothing of what drinking does to the law-making process in Washington and in state capitols. The District of Columbia has the highest alcoholic consumption in the nation, which may explain much which happens there. There is nothing as to why every society has had to regulate the liquor traffic as it has not had to regulate the sale of groceries.

That the money innocently spent for drinks goes into the

bribing of sheriffs and policemen, legislature and judges, never occurred to the writer of the report, to whom Lincoln Steffens' autobiography and the hearings of the Kefauver Committee are unknown. That liquor lobbyists have infested every legislature since colonial days, that the liquor industry is caught with 100,000 crimes a year is unknown. Innocence of the part whiskey plays in government, and not only in this nation, is manifest. The report does not know that whiskey interests worked to put Communists in power because Russia had been dry, or that they helped Hitler in return for wide-open privileges. Mendes-France was removed from being prime minister because he tried to prevent the poisoning of the school children of France by wine.

The report betrays utter ignorance that beer barons make so much more profit than even distillers that they have billions available to break laws or to get them passed and that no state is immune from their continual bribery. In almost every county and city beer is sold to minors and beer joints flourish as centers of crime and debauchery. State highway patrols may be paid for allowing only one brand of beer to be sold in their section. Speakers and lieutenant governors get millions in retainers. One legislator for passing a minor bill was given $50,000 and a retainer of $20,000 a year for the rest of his life. Beer slush funds are so enormous that they are given to most candidates for major office. Beer barons have bribed many legislatures to forbid counties or communities voting on beer and it is forced on them even if few want it. The overwhelming majority of counties in Tennessee have outlawed whiskey but none is permitted to outlaw beer. Any sheriff can get rich by failing to enforce the beer laws. When a county is allowed to vote on beer, the night before beer companies send out trucks to scatter beer cans over the roads to the polls, so people will think there is no use trying to forbid it. The hundreds of counties which have voted out beer find brewers bootleg it in by the truckload. Many beer barons are partners of gangsters and gangsters own many breweries and saloons.

Beer was never drunk by many Americans until the War Department forced it on servicemen in World War II. Often beer was the only drink kept cool. Much drunkenness results from beer and wine and beer can destroy the body and mind as quickly as whiskey. Beer guzzling workers are unlikely to become concerned about exploitation. Beer-drunk adolescents are ripe for riot and lust. Scientists continue to point out that every drink destroys brain cells but the murder goes on.

Nor is there a word about advertising, which spends billions to induce more to become alcoholics. The report does not seem to know that the major profits of the liquor industry do not come from moderate drinkers but from alcoholics; the more alcoholics, the more business. The average alcoholic does not live 10 years; 85% of whiskey is sold to 22% of drinkers, almost all alcoholics. Every alcoholic was first a moderate drinker. Few industries make their money by killing off their best customers. We have the most alcoholics of any nation.

Slippery when wet is evident in these proponents of alcoholism ignoring that most major religions are opposed to drinking and some insist on total abstinence. Gandhi said that he did not mind his son becoming a Christian if it did not mean he had to smoke and drink. In many provinces of India liquor is only allowed to be sold to alleged "Christians." Alcohol is a major charge against whites in Africa and the Orient. Whiskey has been standard in swindling tenants in South Africa or the Arkansas Delta. A fifth is apt to make a tenant forget his fourth. No mention is made how alcohol even in moderation inflames passions and how every race riot begins with drinking. Using groceries in moderation does not result in lynchings.

The liquor industry has paid for whitewashing lies about national prohibition, whence we had the least drinking, the least drunkenness, the fewest drunken drivers, the fewest alcoholics, the fewest gangsters and most institutions closed for lack of patients. The repealers who were seeking to make money and evade taxes promised no saloons, no sale to youth, no liquor ads, no bootlegging, and failed to fulfill one promise. If prohibition had failed, the liquor industry would not have spent billions to buy repeal. Every year more are murdered by drunken drivers, more drinking drivers are arrested, more alcoholics are made, more crimes are committed by those under the influence while more women sell liquor than teach school. Gangsters are the most affluent and powerful in history. Three hundred billion dollars has been wasted by repeal.

Slippery when wet is the argument that saloons reduce taxes. Federal taxes are 50 times what they were under prohibition. Wide-open Nevada has one of the highest tax rates as well as the highest suicide rate. In few states does the whiskey and beer industry pay even its average share of taxes; it pays off instead. Massachusetts noted for years that those taxes did not even take care of the victims of alcohol and a British prime minister offered to abolish taxes on beer and whiskey if the industries would take care of their victims. It is also slippery that you have a right to evade taxes and let the unfortunate alcoholic pay yours.

Slippery when wet is the argument that people drink more when it is illegal; is there a law against smoking? Slippery is the argument that the more whiskey sold, the less will be drunk, and that advertising does not sell more. Slippery when wet is the specious reasoning that any law that can not be perfectly enforced ought to be replaced. Laws have never prevented murder but who advocates legalizing murder? Or stealing, the most frequent law violations? Would less cars be stolen if this were not illegal?

Slippery when wet: that it is easier to control liquor when it is legal, though the industry has never obeyed the law and every month thousands of saloons are caught selling to children. That bootleggers vote for prohibition is another slippery lie; there are more bootleggers in wet territory; it is safer to sell there. A study of precincts shows that the bootlegging precincts vote wet. Slippery when wet is the claim that less liquor is sold with open saloons, which experience proves is untrue. Legally dry Mississippi had the fewest drunken drivers, fewest drunks, alcoholics, fewest crimes connected with alcohol, and most crime was in the counties where the law was least enforced. Repeal doubled our deaths and accidents by drinking drivers. Each year 3 million Americans are injured by drinking drivers; 100 a day are killed by drinking drivers.

Slippery when wet; the whiskey people bought repeal in

87

states and give legislators free whiskey, millions of dollars of retainers and millions in cash to keep people from voting against it. Any House Speaker or lieutenant governor can get all he wants, as can governors, congressmen, legislators, sheriffs. When Mississippi voted for dry law enforcement twice by resounding majorities it was ignored, but a governor elected by drys betrayed them and sold them out. When South Carolina voted dry 25 years ago, the legislature was bribed to ignore it. Although 80% of Tennessee counties are dry, legislators are bribed to keep people from voting on state prohibition. Constitutions of 15 states forbid people voting on liquor. Oklahoma voted dry but enough votes were miscounted in the cities to steal the election and not even the church press published this. Georgia whiskeyrats tried to make it illegal for a county to vote dry, because most Georgia counties have. Sales by the drink produces more profits and more alcoholics, so legislators are bribed to vote for this. The whiskey industry will not be satisfied until it has destroyed our people.

Slippery when wet is the $1 billion spent in bribes to get contracts; almost as much as used in our remarkably unsuccessful diplomacy; alcoholics are in office from White House to courthouse. Whiskey retainers have kept the House of Representatives from voting for years on a bill passed several times by the Senate to forbid the sale of intoxicants on planes, although pilots and stewardesses have begged for the law. How much farther can national insanity get than letting planes crash to sell more whiskey?

Smoking may kill you but it will not drive you insane. Other poisons may end your life but they will not turn you into a dangerous homicidal maniac. Overeating is sinful but it does not cause you to murder your son. "Wine and strong drink take away the understanding," noted the prophet Hosea 2600 years ago. No one has too much sense and alcohol takes away some of what he has. The most sober people will survive. The less intoxicants available, the more sober people there will be, and the safer, kinder, freer, better human life will be.

88

FIFTY YEARS AGO

Fifty years ago a new dawn of hope was dimmed by the tragic failure at Versailles, and more than a generation later we found ourselves at the place in the show where we came in, and seeing it a second time was not as boring as it was terrifying. Was the process just a dream? Is existence a succession of nightmares? Are there no periods in history, just a succession of commas or dashes? Is nothing really ever ended in the human panorama? Are we bound to recapitulate our own mistakes in our own lifetime? This sounded grimmer than any Oriental wheel of fate or series of interminable reincarnations; it called in question all the basic absolutes of the nineteenth century. Yet we learned that after all 1918 had settled nothing except that those who stopped fighting were able to recuperate and fight another day.

We ought not to have been as disillusioned as we were. When Job asked, "Is there not a warfare to man on the earth?", he anticipated the series of conflicts which have made history. Class is more powerful than race or nationality in determining our lives. The class war, the bitterer war of the sexes, the war between the urban and the rural, the incessant conflict between youth and age, dwarf all the dynastic and nationalistic battles which spot the pages of history. Wars are not always won by the more right; God is not a God of battles except in a very long, long run. Those suffering from the neurotic urge to simplify our complex destinies feel more comfortable with a world in which certain dates mark abrupt changes. But many a war has ended in nothing more than an armistice.

The treaty of 1763 banished France from North America and made a simple map of the continent; but it did not prevent a 1963 Canada being more and more influenced by the unchanged French of Quebec. This defeat of the French was only an armistice, for historians have discovered that the French sent agitators to stir up revolutionary fervor in the British colonies almost as soon as they left North America, as an incident in the several hundred years war with Britain. And the French-fed, French-clothed, and French-paid Continentals at

Yorktown with a larger French army and two French fleets watched the reversal of 1763 as the bands played, "The World Turned Upside Down."

We could trace 1783 as an armistice for a war to be resumed on almost the same basis in 1812, and that conflict ended also in an armistice in which neither side obtained what it was fighting for, and the very inconclusiveness of the victory made possible the longest undefended frontiers in the world. An armistice may be better than a victory. Woodrow Wilson was right when he tried after his re-election to obtain a peace without victory, which would have been a long-term armistice. The armistice which closed the Boer War ended in a Boer tyranny much more galling than any British tyranny the trekking Dutch ever endured. The armistice of the cold war has been less tragic than a hot war as the confused world gathers for disagreement in a United Nations.

Only in recent years have some in cooler climes realized that Appomattox was an armistice rather than a victory. By the 1877 deal the South was allowed to win the war racially while the North won it economically and politically. The poor white was ignored in both sections. And now the Second Reconstruction is ending in identical ways, with robber barons bartering away the rights of others to continue exploitation of both races. The burden of integration has again been unloaded on the poor white, while the rich go free. This Reconstruction also began with glowing promises of hope which most Negroes automatically discounted, and correctly. For after the court decisions, executive orders and civil rights legislation, fundamental conditions have not been altered and retreat from reform is again the order of the day.

Southerners learned from losing a conflict that no one is always victorious. Most in other sections have yet to learn that obvious fact of history. The United States may have to lose a war to become mature.

White and black in the South both learned long ago that problems admit of no simple solutions, and this realism is slowly penetrating elsewhere. The sudden trauma of Northerners no longer secure in segregated housing, schooling and working results in hostility accentuated by riots deliberately engineered by reactionary whites to discredit blacks, and by hysterical TV declaring that no man is safe. How far have we come in a century?

Do we have to fight wars, sign armistices and then fight more wars in order to sign more armistices? Are we like the subway crowds jamming by the million down the subways and never told by the ascending throngs that there were no trains running? Have we lost communication? Do we have to repeat the same blunders?

Perhaps we have missed the meaning of November 11. For centuries previous to 1918, the day was held in grateful remembrance by many and commemorated with church services, for November 11 was St. Martin's Day, the center of that autumn splendor known to us as Indian Summer but to Europeans as St. Martin's Summer. St. Martin of Tours was a Roman soldier who became a Christian on the eve of a battle in the year 358. When he refused to fight he was accused of being a coward, but Martin answered "Put me in the forefront of the army, without weapons or armor; but I will not draw sword again. I am become the soldier of Christ." St. Martin is also commemorated on July 4, which may make him a Father of the Revolution. He was also American in that he was elected by the common people who protested when the church authorities were going to select one of their favorites. He was also a predecessor of American Revolutionary thought in that he believed that heretics should not be punished and he refused to meet with his brother bishops who were opposed to freedom of conscience. He preceded our welfare program when he gave his cloak to a beggar, and he was more American when he debunked an old legend by proving that a tomb of a supposed martyr which was the center of religious devotion was really that of a highway robber. St. Martin died in the year 401, but he is much more alive on Armistice Day than John J. Pershing.

If we do not want to join with Catholic Christendom in observing November 11 as St. Martin's Day, there is a more possible commemoration which could come closer to contemporary concerns. We could celebrate November 11 as Kierkegaard

Day, for the great Dane was born on November 11, 1814. Although it might seem that the apostle of either-or was remote from an armistice in thought and deed, as a matter of fact his life was one long armistice broken only by prepared prophetic attacks. His teleological suspension of the ethical is the armistice in which every Christian may engage in when he attempts to serve the present age according to the will of God even if not in accord with the ethics of his age. Humor and poetry were to S. K. armistices in the grim warfare of life, and he availed himself of both. He proved the presence of God by worship rather than by argument: "a truce with controversialists who undertake to prove men into salvation." He regarded himself as a missionary to introduce Christianity into Christendom, and he prepared for that warfare carefully over the years, holding his fire until he saw the whites of his ecclesiastical opponents' eyes. "Neither the individual nor the church is in secure possession of the truth but must continually strive to possess it. Deification of the church is nothing but permanent rebellion against God. There is hardly a nation in Europe or America which does not count itself a Christian nation—especially when it is at war with another."

Kierkegaard wrote that "Each anniversary shall be a solemn holiday, with power in its remembrance and hope in its promise." Is this not true of our Armistice Day, of St. Martin's Day, of the birthday of the one who has recalled many modern thinkers to the Christ beyond the confines of ecclesiasticism? And may we not find in November 11 the significance he found when he wrote: "But he who has fellowship with God lives with One whose presence gives even the most insignificant an infinite significance." The unknown soldier and the unknown saint and the unknown sinner are of eternal worth in the God who is not unknown.

COMES THE MOMENT TO DECIDE

It is a pleasure on the day after the nonpolitical holiday of Confederate Memorial Day to speak to an institution founded with the nonpolitical purpose of rescuing Southerners of 1850 from Northern education under the influence of a church whose connection with a certain Henry is obviously nonpolitical and whose American branch owes its separation to a nonpolitical revolution of 1776. Around a certain book of uncommon prayer lingers the aroma of its adoption by a nonpolitical parliament and the fragrance of amendments by general conventions as remote from politics as from religion. Into this Arcadian atmosphere of insulated ivory towers obviously echoes could not penetrate of unhierarchical remarks about all men being equal even though aided and abetted by an Anglican from Hyde Park and a man of Independence. Into such a status quo it may seem indelicate to inject a few remarks on the relation of what passes for religion to what passes for politics.

It could be gently insinuated that to do nothing in politics is to do something. You may have heard why the priest passed by the man on the Jericho road—the man had already been robbed. Passersby who watch murder without giving alarm may be accomplices and bystanders when pockets are picked may be pals. To be neutral between ignorance and learning is to favor the continuance of ignorance. The isolationist Alabamian was going to stop Hitler the minute he crossed the Georgia line.

We can not fence off from faith vital areas because they are in politics. As William Temple insisted, "God is not only concerned with religion, or even primarily." The ballot box can be as holy as the communion plate. Politics is not all nonecclesiastical; there was more religion in Philadelphia at a political convention in 1948 and more politics at a church convention in 1946. Religious and educational politics are more crooked because they have no opposition party to expose them.

Politics is how we do together what we can not do separately. Democracy is the faith that no one is good enough to tell others what they have to do. The only alternative to politics is dictatorship. As Chesterton insists, democracy is based

93

on original sin: there are no "good people," though there are better and worse. Politicians do not bribe each other; business men bribe them. When ministers go into politics for the status quo, you hear no objection. Leslie Glenn told Francis Sayre, the grandson of Woodrow Wilson, at his ordination that we need 100 Christian wardheelers more than 100 Sunday School teachers.

No man is better than his information, but the average church member never realizes that he only hears one party's side through press and screen. Like the average man outside of the church, he never discovers that back of nation and state government is the invisible government of a few families and back of most local government is the invisible government of organized crime. The average Protestant church member belongs to their party and never realizes it is responsible for the obscene screen, pornographic press and narcotics traffic. He never realizes how often organized crime determines presidents, senators, governors, judges, district attorneys nor how it controls legislative committees. He did not note that an attorney general and governor who never disturbed gangsters in a gangster-ridden state became chief justice. We are not allowed to know who murdered a president because it would uncover major criminals. No wonder only 1 of 25 gangsters arrested comes to court and less than 1 of 100 serve time.

Cosa Nostra is part of the national crime syndicate which has been growing in power ever since the repeal of prohibition, which temporarily reduced its profits of pre-prohibition days. Organized crime makes $50 billion a year through gambling, loansharking, vice, narcotics, saloons, extortion, murder. It will murder almost anyone for $5,000. Organized crime controls professional and college ball teams, wrestling, boxing, racetracks, singers, entertainers. Gangsters steal from the poor more than the government donates to them. Every day we pay unconscious toll to the syndicate, which runs thousands of legitimate businesses. Most Protestants voted in 1920 for Warren G. Harding, whose loathsome private life they never learned and who let crime organize. In more recent years they have helped gangsters take over the White House again.

The king's henchman told Micaiah, "Behold now, the words of the prophets declare good with one mouth: let your word, I beg you, be like the word of one of them and speak that which is good," Micaiah replied, "As the Lord lives, what the Lord says unto me, that will I speak." We are back again with the brave answer of Micaiah, who lived almost 3,000 years ago but who is our contemporary who walks our ways today. The Word of the Lord comes to us to give to others and we can not give into agreeing with false prophets. No prophet left foreign policy to stupid presidents, muddleheaded militarists, senile senators. My name has been Micaiah, as has been that of every faithful witness for the Eternal. As the Lord lives, what He tells us to speak, that must we speak. We can do no other.

> It is part of the daily duty and a large and important part of every preacher's office to give fearlessly to all men and to all actions their absolutely right names.

So declared Alexander Whyte, one of the great Scottish preachers of the last century. As one of the first in the South to warn of the menace of Hitler, I marvel how many in our country are sound asleep to the deadlier dangers of our homegrown Hitlers, drugged by the hallucination that it can't happen here. The same stupidity and ignorance led many German ministers and church members to vote for Hitler. The average American Protestant votes for our Hitlers. Like the Germans, he swallows the false charges that those who work for democracy are Communists, never opening his eyes to discover that only democratic leaders oppose the dictatorship of Communists and that Communists always support the enemies of democracy. The church member slides over the parable of inasmuch without ever dreaming that Jesus could be speaking of him when Jesus declares that those who fail to help the poor doom themselves to endless destruction.

The Biblical prophet was never a professional evangelist betraying the gospel to cruel exploiters saturated with lust and lies, who leaves God when he makes his first million and who yelps against arrogance, greed and falsehood without ever looking in a mirror.

Even as King Ahaz in the Bible story ruined his nation by falling down before the idols of the nation he had defeated, so every year we get more like Hitler's Germany. Hitler won the war as we follow his footsteps by rearming Nazis for another world war while they arm Red China. We have given Germany $100 billion, the most ever given to any nation. We waste billions needed at home to keep in power the cruel murderers of Spain who helped Hitler sink our ships. We arm the South Vietnamese dictator who worships Hitler, the Korean traitor on Hitler's side whom we put in power, the Paraguayan and Brazilian Nazi dictators, while treasonable Americans who took the side of Hitler hold high office.

Hitler took over Germany after an election in which he was financed by robber barons, including leading American Republicans. Stealing of votes by gangsters and a third party put him in power. He was helped into power by a decade of riots, vice, crime, oceans of lies against democracy, deliberate sabotage of democracy, inflation which wiped out the middle class. Hitler prevented another election by a fake Red scare. He murdered those who had opposed him, insisted on network lies every day, spent billions while frantically demolishing health, education and welfare. He increased taxes, prices, crime, immorality, broke down the home and the church and bribed some church leaders to lie for him.

Hitler kept thousands of gaudy guards to protect him, sent stormtroopers to murder opponents, corrupted the courts. His gestapo shadowed every critic and terror was normal. Goering was his attorney general to line up gangsters for him while Goebbels was his hatchet man of lies and vice. He was unable to get along with those who bought his election and he locked himself in his room in raging mania. Press and radio became captive liars, transportation and communication broke down, mail was controlled. Sinister shadows stole billions and to cover up the failure of his police state Hitler began a foreign war allegedly for freedom but in violation of every law of God and man. Has any of this happened to us?

How could church members fail to discover what Speaker Sam Rayburn called "the cruelest face that ever came to Congress?" Or to heed the words of Robert Taft that he was "mean and vindictive," or of Thomas Dewey that he used the methods of Hitler and Stalin? Or that he felt at home visiting murderous Franco? How could they fail to notice that Communists fomented riots to help him and the Viet Cong fought for his victory? Why did church members fail to read the Word of the Lord, the pages of history, the record of character assassination, swindling, cheating, lying, devoid of justice, mercy, truth? An American Hitler is 1,000 times as dangerous, because he has 1,000 times the power. Huey Long said that when Hitlerism came here, it would call itself Americanism.

How have church members failed to observe how crime skyrockets as gangsters control more of our government? Why do they not realize Rebozo does not run a Sunday School and that the Bahamas are a gangster hideout of drunken vice? Hitler did not live on narcotics and whiskey or make foreign headlines by consorting with prostitutes. How can any fail to notice freedom dwindles every day as data banks threaten us, spies shadow us and the gains of a century in government are sold out to sinister criminals intent on 1984 here? How could any fail to notice that gangster stealing of 118,000 votes determined the presidency? Why can't any see why he would try to steal the 1972 election? German church leaders were blind also.

Why has no church leader noted that he was nominated by 666, the mark of the Beast in Revelation? The Beast called down fire from heaven, recovered from political defeat, murdered the honest, required his mark to buy and sell. Why is he so afraid of hearing the gospel that he has set up a state church, with hireling false prophets, such as Micaiah and Amos denounced? How could a church read in services instead of the Bible the words of Richard the Lyinhearted? How much farther can blasphemy go?

The Biblical way is not the way of labor-baiting Rehoboams or of profiteering Jeroboams but of the welfare in the wilderness, the democracy in the desert, the democratic revolution of the dispossessed under David. The last line in the historical books extols one who sought the welfare of his people and

97

psalm and proverb praise political care for the poor. How can we follow the prophets if we do not enter into politics—Amos exposing the injustice of dictators and exploiters, Hosea more concerned with mercy than churchgoing, Jeremiah defining faith as helping the needy, Isaiah insisting worship demands justice? And Jonah thundering against isolationism ecclesiastical as well as national, Zechariah urging homes for the old and playgrounds for the young, Malachi demanding brotherhood under one common Father? How can we stay out of politics and bring the good news to the poor or pass the final examination of Jesus on Inasmuch?

In this room I learned words which have inspired my ministry through the years.

Once to every man and nation comes the moment to decide
In the strife of truth or falsehood for the good or evil side . . .
Then it is the brave man chooses, while the coward stands
*   aside.*
Till the multitude make virtue of the faith that they denied.
By the light of burning martyrs Jesus' bleeding feet I track
Toiling up new Calvaries ever with the cross that turns not
*   back.*

Though the cause of evil prosper, yet 'tis truth alone is strong,
Though her portion be the scaffold and upon the throne be
*   wrong,*
Yet that scaffold sways the future, and behind the dim unknown
Standeth God within the shadow, keeping watch above His own.

THE GIFT GETS LOST IN THE WRAPPINGS

The gift gets lost in the wrappings. Has this ever happened to you at Christmas? It has to others. And they either had to go through all the wrappings again to find the missing gift, or they discovered the present had been accidentally thrown away.

Has your real Christmas become lost in the wrappings? It has for many people. Christmas is not a moral holiday, not a saturnalia, not an occasion of alcoholism and gluttony, nor of selfish giving and more selfish receiving. The Philistines are still at Bethlehem. For some the Christmas star has been replaced by a bottle of poison, while unwise men are deluded into bringing for Christmas liquids which destroy eternal life. During one Christmas season, *Life* carried 128 pages of whiskey lies, the *New Yorker* 222 pages, *Time* 71, *Newsweek* 89, *News Report* 59, *Look* 51, *Ebony* 51, *Holiday* 48. Every year many die from the results of alcohol on Christmas. Has Christ been lost in poisoning our fellowmen? One drink can turn a joyous family gathering into a night of horror. The gift has been thrown away in the wrappings.

Nor does the wrapping have to be something evil. Annually we spend $50 million on Christmas trees, $90 million on decorations, $450 million on toys. These are good, but this is more than we give in 12 months to spread the gospel of the One who was born at this time. We spend more on airconditioning churches than on giving the good news to the world.

The green of Christmas gets lost in the wrappings. Hosea noted that he was like an evergreen tree in the sight of the Lord. Trees that stay green all year have a symbolism for the Christian. The tree is a lovely part of the season. But decorations on the tree may make us forget that the gift which we have never received may be waiting for us at the tree. At the tree is rest for the weary soul, calm for the troubled heart. The peace that a bewildered world seeks by bombs comes here by brotherhood; the light which gleams on our tree is no transient light.

Christmas is for the undereducated and the overeducated but not for the halfeducated. It is for those who know they do not know and for those who know they know but not for those who do not know that they do not know. The gift came with songs to shepherds. They were uneducated and underpaid union labor, but they were wise. Simple and childlike folk, the humble, the meek, the penitent can receive the gift. The gift came to sages with stars and to seers with a Savior. The overeducated wise men could also find the way. Only those whom a little learning inflates are hurt by it. Wisdom leads to truth. There is a silver star in every life, which if we follow, leads to Bethlehem. The star makes life anew a fair design of wonder and of joy.

The white of the Christmas message may get lost in the white wrappings. God is more in snow than in flowers or trees. He sends the snow, which covers the imperfections of earth as his love covers our sins, and makes radiant the drab earth as His grace does our dull days. The whiteness of God's snow prepares for the emerald of spring, as He moves in a mysterious way His wonders to perform. Ever new and fresh from the hand of God is each snowflake in a different design from the Author of symmetry and Lover of varied beauty. The snow falls as softly as the great gifts of God, as silently as He enters our hearts.

> *White as the prayers of Mary*
> *The silent flakes drift down,*
> *Like angel hosts descending*
> *Upon the little town.*
> *Immaculate as Jesus*
> *Is the earth's new spotless gown.*
> *White as the prayers of Mary*
> *The*
>   *silent*
>   *flakes*
>   *drift*
>   *down.*

The red of the holly berries is the scarlet dawn of a better day, a deeper red than other revolutions. The Child in the manger began a new underground, a revolution against the princes of this world, to put down the mighty, exalt the humble and meek and send the rich empty away. He turns the world upside down until it comes right side up. Herod and his councils were correct on fearing this dangerous birth. Before the red revolution of Jesus shall prejudice crash, pride totter, and exploitation fall.

Some who heard the first message of peace and good will were sore afraid. Millions today are afraid of peace and good will. What would good will do to manufacturers of inflammable clothes for babies, of deadly toys for children, of fireworks that blind and maim? Savonarola wrote: "Unless good will is found among you, you can not have peace." What would good will do to hearts heavy with hate, faces sharp with malice cold? What would peace do to profiteers and Pentagons in all lands? Is there still no room in the inn? How can a gangster senator hating peace record carols? Christ will not come to a white house or any other house of hate until He comes in flaming judgment on those who live by hate, greed, lust and lies. Appropriate was the Christmas stamp which pictured an angel with a trumpet, because we live between the trumpet of the angel of Bethlehem and the trumpet of the angel of judgment.

> *Beneath the angels' song have rolled*
> *Two thousand years of wrong.*

Twenty-five, 26, 27, 28 is no inconsequential sequence. As Thomas à Becket pointed out in his last sermon, St. Stephen's is the day after Christmas, the commemoration of the birth of Christ is followed by the remembrance of the death of His first martyr, the witness of the Apostle John on the 27th, by the murder of the Holy Innocents on the 28th. Birth and death, dawn and dusk, cradle and cross are inextricably entwined. The evil who murdered the innocents and the witnesses of good will are still in power, but they do not have the last word. We remember the stoned Stephen, the John of Patmos, the Holy Innocents. The message of 25, 26, 27, 28 is that love is eternally victorious.

The gift is still waiting at the tree. The green of eternal life, the white of peace, the red of courage await you, if you will turn to Him remembering the day the world began anew.

> *How shall we love Thee, holy hidden Being,*
> *If we love not the world which Thou hast made?*
> *O give us brother love for better seeing,*
> *Thy Word made flesh and in a manger laid.*
> *Thy kingdom come, O Lord, Thy will be done.*

AND THE RIVER ROSE

Matthew 7:25

"And the river rose." So Norlie graphically expresses it, in the most readable American version. Those who have lived by rivers recognize the very real picture. The river rose, the flood came, the house fell.

The laws of the universe do not threaten, they operate. Electricity does not warn you not to touch the hot wire, fire does not threaten to burn you, gravitation does not advise you not to jump.

Jesus does not give advice or recommendations; He tells you these are the laws of life which you will obey if you use your intelligence. Jesus does not say that you will follow His teaching if you are religious or moral but if you do not want your life to collapse when the river rises.

A life built on status will go to pieces. Millions of status seekers try to fool others with status signs, showy cars, garish clothing, conspicuous waste, suburban showplaces, vacuous fraternities, country club churches. But they fool no one; their lack of status is clear from their frantic urge to claim it. The only real status is to be on the solid rock of faith. It was written of a Princeton dean that because he knew God loved him and Christ died for him, he did not need any reassurance about his importance.

A life built on dishonesty will collapse. Sham is sand, false fronts will be exposed; only the true will stand when the river rises. A house built with shoddy materials goes to pieces; so does such a life. Dishonesty gets to be evident on the face that no one trusts. The river has risen and the house on the sand is gone.

We have all observed how quickly a life based on a bottle collapses. Refusal to face reality is the shiftiest of sands. More lives crash from this in our land than in any other. We have more saloons than churches and spend five times as much on the former. Look at the empty face of the alcoholic and see what whiskey and beer have made of him, how they have dehumanized him. The river has risen and life has gone to pieces. No life based on immorality can stand when the river rises. Any life will cave in which refuses to recognize the sacredness of another human personality. Exploiting another destroys you. Those who fail to recognize the deeps of another personality make their own more shallow. Disintegration of a person results from lust.

A life built on hate will collapse when the river rises. Hate hurts the hater most. When the apostle wrote "Alexander the coppersmith did me much evil; the Lord will reward him according to his works," he was making a realistic observation of a certainty. Hate of Catholics and Jews is unAmerican; so is hate of Protestants, which is bitter and widespread. Hate of blacks is destructive; so is hate of whites. Civil rights are also for whites. There is no civil right to commit civil wrong. Belgians who cut off the hands of thousands of Congolese for not bringing in enough rubber were repaid two generations later. Jesus warned it is better to jump in the ocean with a millstone about your neck than to hurt a little child. A universe which does not tolerate material deviations of one-millionth of an inch does not tolerate moral deviation.

The river will rise on any life centering around the organized insanity of the screen and it will go to pieces. Civilization consisted in rising from a picture with one meaning to a word which is worth 1,000 pictures. Only the primitive and the infantile live by pictures. But the problem is much more serious than the narrowness of pictures; the real problem is what pictures are presented on our screens. Television could bring us wonderful church services, uplifting music, poetry which reaches the deeps of the human heart, an understanding of how to make the home a haven of hope, consideration of what goes on in the spirit of Jesus. It could educate millions, could free from superstition and savagery, could show us how to walk in the shining light.

But it does none of these. TV is much more dangerous to civilization than hydrogen missiles, which only destroy the body. Although the air belongs to the American people, it is controlled by traitors who are rapidly destroying our liberty and our life. TV poisons the body but much more the mind and soul.

No people ever were so enslaved as those whose eyes are glued to the idiot box, whose world is its screen. Foreign dictators wish they had such complete control of what people see and hear. No slavery is more helpless than of those drugged by TV. Thomas Jefferson said he felt sorry for people who read newspapers, because they would never know what was going on in their lifetime. When Kierkegaard said of the daily paper "Here men are demoralized in the quickest way," he could not envision television. News includes glaring omissions, outright lies and infantile irrelevancies. Not one commentator dares tell you what happens in one day. Much news is manufactured and never occurs. To reduce world problems to personalities deludes ignorance. Emotions drained off hourly by TV are not available when needed for the deep problems of life.

Mentalities permanently arrested by Westerns in which the good guys ride white horses and win by violence and Northerns in which crime never pays become incapable of understanding the complexities of living. TV addicts let the idiot box determine what and when they eat and believe. Fortifying natural mental indolence and feeblemindedness chronic to the human race makes it more servile to exploiters. TV has crippled conversation, almost eliminated reading, wrecked thinking. Addicts become puppets manipulated by strings producing a bumper crop of gullibles. Any halfwit or murderer can be made a hero in a few days. Incumbents are fortified by free time and you can not buy time on TV to expose major criminals. Elections are for sale to the one with the most money to come into your home more often and the honest are deliberately kept out of sight by the completely Republican networks. Remember the deliberate distortion of the Chicago convention?

No one is as close to Jesus after an evening with TV and constant gawking at it may vaccinate permanently against the Eternal. Covetousness is hawked as happiness and false advertising picks your pocket. Poor children are cruelly exposed to luxury they can never hope to have. Stealing is standard and a 4-year-old girl has seen murder and indecency thousands of times. No generation ever had such a handicap. Adultery steadily on the screen warps minds, wrecks homes. Murder and violence are taught by thousands of repetitions. Riots are deliberately staged to start more riots. TV created the generation gap by keeping youth from reading and replacing sanity and responsible freedom with insane hatred of parents. The day of worship is profaned into a day of huckstering, insanity and lust, the name of the Eternal is used in vain and the idiot box becomes the idol which takes first place in time. Producers of TV intend to destroy faith in God and man and these enemies of our country and our faith have almost succeeded. For God's sake, shut up—your TV set!

A life or a country built on arrogance will crash. The Almighty has not given the world to one nation nor did He authorize us to pollute another planet in larger lunacy. World War II wrecked us when we took over the militaristic arrogance we defeated. It is insufferable arrogance to store up bacteria and poison for reservoirs, arrogance to waste $1 trillion on defense which can not defend. It is arrogance to bring slow death into a community, to murder by food or drink, to sell cancer, to pollute imaginations and poison minds. The Eternal did not give us the right to use up most of the world's production. No nation ever spent so much time and money going round and round. Our arrogant industries have devastated our land, destroyed our forests, polluted our rivers, poisoned the very air we breathe.

The river has risen on our national life and we are going down faster than Rome did. We have followed the Roman road from monarchy to oligarchy to democracy to military dictatorship. Rome fell by wasting its strength on remote wars while letting in hordes of barbarians, by profiteering monopolies and spiraling inflation, by drugs and drunkenness, divorce and race suicide, obscenity and perversion, vice and crime, military dictators crushing with an iron hand and giving free games to watch. Thomas Macaulay observed a century ago

> Your country will be pillaged in the 20th century by barbarians just as the Roman Empire was in the 5th century, but with the difference that your devastation will be from your own country, the product of your own misdeeds.

The river is rising ominously over American life. Our country is falling to pieces before our eyes. The accelerating deterioration of American life makes it improbable the liberty of 1776 will be here by 1976; 1984 has come here way ahead of time. Our cities are jungles of terror as deliberately engineered violence takes away our liberty and life. White criminals finance black vandalism to destroy liberty for black and white. Our homes, our schools, our jobs, our churches have been taken from us.

Truth is hidden from us as in Russia and history distorted. Products disappear from shelves and people from our lives in increasing depersonalization. Our postal system is destroyed that we may not communicate and rigged polls try to eliminate voting. We are fed falsehood and bombarded by supersonic sound and raucous noise to keep us from hearing. We owe $3 trillion to giant corporations who make $200 billion yearly while we pay the same in swollen taxes. Credit cards bite our pockets and inflation, Republican taxation without representation, destroys security. More are in hospitals for the mind than for the body and hectic commercialized Sundays leave us more neurotic. Emerson said that free institutions would go when Sunday goes and our day of rest has been sabotaged by those who hate the Protestant faith which made us free.

The deliberate degradation of girls and boys is to extinguish hope, the enticement to narcotics are to enslave, as is the organized breakdowns of moral standards. Movie-mad and TV-twisted children are rendered incapable of learning, which has disappeared from most campuses with decency and culture. A pervert mafia keeps pervert college presidents in power. We are losing the real civil war to anarchists and the sinister shadows behind them ready to enslave us. A moral chain reaction can destroy as rapidly as a nuclear. The river will rise over any nation which worships Baal, Ashtaroth, Moloch.

Any church which does not build on the teachings of Jesus will crash when the river rises. The house of God is meant to be a place to exchange the turmoil of the day for the tranquillity of the eternal. But so often is it a den of thieves that God commanded Hosea to set a trumpet against the church and Amos to smite and smash it, while Paul evaluated the church at Corinth "When you come together, you do more harm than good."

Church machines can be more merciless and ruthless than political rings. Members preferring bricks to souls shell out millions for big barns and dole out pennies for missions. A village in Ceylon could be fed from the cost of a stained-glass window and the millions spent on freezing church air could bring the gospel to all. No rich man is so rotten some church will not take his money and promise fire insurance for the next world. Church editors approve poisoning reservoirs and infecting children with bacteria. In stained-glass jungles cruel-eyed evangelists whitewash lustful hatemongers and thieving bishops are alcoholic perverts. In *Sesame and Lilies,* John Ruskin observed

> Bishops will be punished for every help withheld, for every truth refused, for every falsehood enforced.

Gladstone stated that the church would part with her faith before her finance.

Dishonest religion which misleads you that you can buy your way into heaven or negotiate it by some formal observance is shifting sand on which you will collapse. The Judge does not authorize shortcuts and the decision of the Judge will be final. Nothing really matters in life but Jesus. Only when you have built your life on His words are you on the solid rock.

AT THE END OF THE ROAD YOU MEET GOD

As you ride the high road from Virginia into Kentucky, through the gap where the brave pioneer and the gray raider came, you see this sign: "At the end of the road you meet God."

Roadside signs do not usually impress, but this does. On the curving mountain road 3,000 feet high, by precipices and deep hollows, it is extremely appropriate to be reminded that at the end of the trail you meet God. If you imbibe some of the legal poison sold nearby to enrich criminals, you may meet

Him quicker and unprepared. Some have made this a black Christmas for many. Jesus warned that it is better to drown yourself in the ocean than to cause one of God's little ones to go astray. At the end of the road—God!

You can't get away from God. What in the world makes you think you can? You simpleminded Jonah! Where can you flee from His Presence? Can you get away from God by darkness or light, by night or day, by hiding at home or flying to the ends of the universe? As the writer of Deuteronomy advised long ago, "If they were wise, they would understand, they would consider their last end." At the end—God!

You can try to get away by alcohol, but there is always the morning after and you have to face yourself—and God. Drugs are an escape that does not last. You can stay away from church, stay up late Saturday so you will be sleepy Sunday morning, turn off religious radio programs—but you have not escaped the Eternal. You can spend your Sundays running from God in field or forest, on the road or the lake or the golf course, but you will find no escape from God; He is there.

You can deaden yourself to the finer things in life by lust and cruelty, but you have not thereby escaped God. To keep from thinking or looking at the Bible you may read trash by the hour, but you have not gotten away from the Eternal. You can take the easy way out of becoming a slave to an idiot screen but you have not escaped God. There is no TV in a hearse. A hearse in Colorado has the appropriate number— U 2. You can soak your mind in the evil provocations of movies, but you come out again into the clean air—and there is God.

You can run away from ministers and teachers, from friends and family who try to bring you closer to God, but you can never escape remembering. In every home you will be reminded of God. Science pursued to its inevitable conclusions will take you to the Eternal Architect of all things visible and invisible. The pages of history will read as a counterpoint melody His Story. Poetry will summon you to the Eternal Poet. As Browning wrote

Just when we're safest, there's a sunset touch,
A fancy from a flowerbell, someone's death,
A chorus ending from Euripides,
And that's enough for fifty hopes and fears. . . .
The good God, what He could do if He would,
Would if He could, then must have done long since.

At the end of the road you meet God. The inescapable Jesus faces you on every avenue of living. In life it is more important whom you know than what you know. On the highway of life it is not what you know but Whom. At the end of the road you meet Him. At the end of the year you meet Him. At the end of the day you meet Him. Don't you want to meet Him today, as Friend? Say with Sidney Lanier

And you myself, lastly Thee,
God, Whom all roads reach, where'er they run,
My Father, Friend, Beloved, dear-All-One,
Thee in my soul, my soul in Thee.

At the end of every road you meet God, of the road or days or of destiny, of starlight or of song. At the end of the road you encounter the Eternal. Every man has met God at the end of his road. Some like Enoch have walked home with God. We all know that there is a Judge at the end of the long years, the weary years. But that we might know Him better before we come to the end of the road, the Light of life came down to Bethlehem. Jesus came to make clearer the way to God. He came that we might know God as friend before we meet Him as Judge. Then shall we know Him, and not as a Stranger. This is the promise at the end of the road.

Still shines in the darkness the light that gleamed for starry-eyed seekers, for simple shepherds, for sincere saints. Bethlehem was the end of the road for the wise men and they met God there. It was the end of the road for the shepherds and they saw God there. The saintly souls recognized Him Whom they had known all their lives because they had walked with Him all their years. Because He walked our weary ways and shared our dusty days, we know Him, and not as a Stranger. At the end of the road we shall meet the same God Who walks with us today.

WHO IN HELL IS BACK OF ALL THIS?

Who in hell is back of all this? How did our world get in such horrible shape? Why is our country going to pieces before our eyes? Why are our own lives so filled with frustration and tragedy? Why does everything seem to go wrong, in the little matters as well as the big? Why is good so fragile, evil so hard to end? Why do those who do the work never get ahead? What prevents a land of overproduction from ending poverty? Why is it so hard to be honest, true, pure, kind?

Who is responsible for wars, slums, concentration camps? Who is the author of exploitation, murder, shame? Who in hell would give cancer to mothers? Who breaks homes, debauches youth, warps lives? Who decides what we can read? Who picks out our movies and TV programs? Who keeps us from finding out the truth? Who manages to get people of good intentions fighting each other instead of fighting evil? Is there a sadistic malevolence in the universe?

No one has pondered deeply the problems of human living until he has discovered the almost overwhelming power of evil. Evil is too strong, too well organized, too resilient, too pervasive, to be merely a fortuitous combination of circumstances. Add the letter "d" to evil and you get devil.

Most of the American people, like most people in most ages, do not worship the true and living God, but rather the world, the flesh, the devil, otherwise known as greed, lust and hate, and in the Old Testament as the idols which ruined ancient Israel and Judah, Baal, Ashtaroth and Moloch. Jeremiah warned those who imagined they could fool the Eternal:

> Behold, you trust in lying words that can not profit; will you steal, murder, commit adultery, burn incense to Baal and walk after other gods, and stand in My house?

The worship of the Almighty Dollar is the worship of Baal. We are the first people feebleminded enough to let ourselves be bombarded every hour by shrill urges to buy, buy, buy. Baal segregates by cash only; he paid back with property those who paid off his purchasable priests. Only the religion of Baal was fashionable in the country club of Jerusalem. Ostentatious genuflections to Baal run from Wall Street, the center of Baal worship, to Main Street, where devotees drive 100 miles to make up missing a worship of Baal who will not drive 5 blocks to worship the Eternal. Baal turned the day of rest into a day of clamorous huckstering.

Witchcraft was undiluted Baalism in which narcotics and terror were used. Baal is the deity of those who will murder you for a nickel. Baal is the deity of our city jungles. For Baal we have worn out the soil, stripmined the hills, devastated the forests, polluted the water, poisoned the very air we must breathe.

The cult of the shiny new car, for which millions sacrifice better things, is a token of Baalism. Millions doom themselves to financial slavery to be misled by a meaningless new model. The car is the center of many lives, though we are crippled by unsafe construction, swindled by overpriced gimmicks, poisoned by noxious fumes. Our day of rest is given to the car; no people ever spent so much time going round and round. Crime and vice are accentuated by it and the cult of conspicuous waste requires children to be initiated into this wasteful worship.

"Thou shalt steal" was the creed of the party of Baal in the days of Elijah and Amos and it has not changed making the rich richer and the poor poorer. Baal was the deity of exploiting the poor, hating labor, resenting any security or help for the common man. A tall idol on our capitol grounds incarnates hate for labor.

The prophet motive is the opposite of the profit motive. Millions of church members fail to realize that they belong to the contemporary reincarnation of the party of Baal. It was sheer Baalism when Calvin Coolidge whined "The business of this country is business," when Charles Wilson dictated "What is good for General Motors is good for the country," when Herbert Hoover vetoed food for the hungry while signing a bill to give food to cattle. Baalism reduces government to a giveaway to Big Business. Our taxation is of Baal, as the poor pay on every penny they spend while the rich are not taxed on the millions they own.

Baal has taken over war from Moloch and stealing blood money is more important in war than killing. We draft men but not money. Baal worshippers prefer nerve and germ warfare because it only kills people, it does not damage property. We issue bonds so that the poor will pay for the war several times to bloated bondholders. In 1940 our major industries went on strike and refused to produce arms to defend us until the law allowing only 10% profit on arms was repealed. They stayed on a sitdown strike for a year until that law was repealed. When Franklin D. Roosevelt limited wartime incomes to $25,000, Congress promptly overrode him to make the world safe for plutocracy. Baal is lord on Capitol Hill.

Worshippers of Baal do not intend for their children to know any other faith and will run out of town anyone who teaches or preaches against Baal, as they did Elijah and Amos. The trained dogs of Baal know when to bark, the highly-advertised priests, the evangelists clamoring for cash, the peddlers of religious sleeping pills, the congealed cowardly conformists. Baalites worship Baal six days a week, not just one hour; but on the other day they take out fire insurance against the improbability that Baal will ever fail them.

Our worship of Moloch begins when we indelibly imprint terror and violence on the impressionable minds of babies and let horror warp their imaginations. We murder by sport and car and pollution. Hate sharply etched on cruel faces gets power by urging more hate.

We shudder when we read of the ancient worshippers of Moloch throwing their little babies on the red-hot altar of Moloch to be burned alive. But we burn more babies with flame from the skies, murder more infants with fallout, draft our sons to be burned alive. We prepare pestilence by storing bacteria of incurable plagues, poison for reservoirs and cylinders each of which can kill a million people. Highways and railways bristle with explosives and sudden death comes from our own missiles. We are the first capable of ending human life and have some insane enough to risk it.

We spend $30 for Moloch for each $1 for Jesus. No military in Germany or Rome ever held such power. I used to predict every New Year that Russia would not attack us, because it had more to lose. But the lies of the cold war by generals on both sides wasted $1 trillion and warped millions of lives by a draft to make more generals and to pay servicemen less. The most prepared nations lost the world wars and we are so over-prepared we can not win a jungle war even by massacre.

The Pentagon determines war or peace, dictates our foreign policies, entrenches murderous dictators in power, arms and overthrows governments, determines presidents, coerces Congress through spending, donates hundreds of billions to profiteers, arrogates to itself most of our resources and takes every dollar of income tax and $50 billion more a year, while giving us no real defense. It is the largest subsidizer of obscene movies and is responsible for millions of narcotic addicts and alcoholics. The world hates it for encouraging torture and making millions of prostitutes.

Ashtaroth, the goddess of adultery, specialized in broken bodies, broken homes, broken hearts, broken lives. No land has ever been free from this loathsome cult but the unashamed worship of the obscene Ashtaroth was brought here early in this century by scum purveyors of filth from the Mediterranean where the cult never ended. As the Orontes flowed into the Tiber and poisoned Rome, so have we been poisoned, and we are in worse shape than Rome because it had no screen or print to multiply obscenity into every home.

The horrible homebreaking of Hollywood has given us the most broken homes in the world. The open exploitation of feeble-minded and drugged girls is not confined to the prostitute state of Nevada, run by cruel gangsters, but its hideous and appalling inhumanity is in every state. Loathsome disease skyrockets as millions of adolescents are debauched. When only the Pope warns us that we can no more bypass biology than we can bypass Jesus, we are in sad shape. The cult of Ashtaroth is marked by lurid magazines, leering songs, demoralizing caco-

113

phony, filthy novels, inciting dances, provocative dress, sensual cosmetics, savage jewelry, vulgar display, lustful beaches, indecent advertising, a stage so rotten that it only survives by tax subsidies. Our exploitation of women in other lands makes us hated by billions. A civilization which debauches its future mothers will perish. The eminent French philosopher, Jacques Maritain, observes "All our civilization is of Ashtaroth."

Hypnotized by screens, unable to think or read, millions are demoralized, brutalized, paralyzed, debauched and degraded. Television is only a little less lustful than movies, where nothing is too rotten to be exploited. Adult movies mean adulterous movies, drive-ins are dens of sordid shame. I was too young to realize that the first talking movie was a vicious attack on the religion of the Old Testament in favor of Ashtaroth. What of a nation which tolerates horror movies driving children insane?

The movie world of rape, seduction, adultery and sodomy, even uses Bible titles to wreck faith in God. The purpose of movies is not as much to make money as to produce perverts and prostitutes, to wreck the home, to make girls and boys, men and women into slaves of fiendish cruelty and lustful exploitation. Films deliberately glamorize crime and incite to it, as they did to drinking under prohibition. Most actors are prostitutes, perverts, scum. Children schooled in vice and crime are crippled for life mentally and emotionally. As Rudyard Kipling observed

And here come hired youths and girls who feign to love and sin,
In tones like rusty razorblades to tunes like smitten tin,
And here is mock of faith and truth for children to behold
And every door of ancient dirt reopened to the old.

Movies are made on the submoronic level. Will Rogers noted long ago that if education did not destroy the movies, they would destroy education. Why has no one been jailed for blasphemous attacks on Protestant churches, on the Bible, on God? "Surely this iniquity shall never be forgiven you, says the Lord."

The mark of the Beast, Baal, Moloch, Ashtaroth, is upon our faces and fashions. Slick magazines which promise life bring death along with moron digests while TV aerials mark homes open at all hours to the unholy three. Israel and Judah doomed themselves to utter destruction by the worship of Baal, Ashtaroth, Moloch. The same fate awaits us. Will the Judge who comes to judge the quick and the dead find you worshipping this unholy trinity or the Trinity of hope, faith and love? The coming Christ comes with a new age of justice and peace. "Even so, come, Lord Jesus."

AS IT WAS IN THE BEGINNING?

"What must I do to be saved?" shouted the excited jailer. "Now, let's look at this together," answered Paul; "Just what is your viewpoint on salvation in its contemporary connotations?"

And Cornelius said, "Now just tell us what the Lord hast told you." But Peter rejoined: "The day of authoritarian teaching has passed; let's discuss the possibilities of gradual adjustment of ethnic relationships, and at what foreseeable future date mutuality may emerge out of the realm of possibility into the realm of probability. Paradoxical as it may seem to you, sometimes the best way to approach the subject is to talk over our varying viewpoints rather than rush into precipitate action."

And they said, "Brethren, what shall we do?" But Peter stood up and responded, "Men and brethren, to say what we shall do is to adopt an activism unjustified by the existential environment. This is no place for dictatorial decisions or for rehearsing the slogans of the past. Let's divide up into buzz groups of fifteen and then come together to see what we have found by this dynamic process."

"May we know what this new teaching is?" politely inquired the delegation from the Society for the Advancement of Constructive Thinking of Mars Hill, Incorporated. "Delighted," chuckled Paul; "In a metropolis with so many diverse viewpoints, it is obvious that we have many resource leaders available. I propose that we discuss the deities of Athens, and that

115

you let me have a few minutes to present my point of view, of course, as one among many."

Now when he reasoned of justice, self-control, and coming judgment, Felix became indignant and remarked, "Obviously, what you are presenting is just your own personal predilection, without the corrective norm of group observation. We shall have a panel discussion, with audience participation, on these controversial subjects."

And King Agrippa remonstrated, "But you are in too much of a hurry to make into a Christian." "By no means," apologized Paul deferentially; "I was just opening the matter for further consideration, so that at our next meeting we can see what group reactions can do to channel the approaches to this very interesting matter on experiences along the highway. Why, King Agrippa, you doubtless have had some interesting experiences along the toll road to Damascus which would enlighten us all."

And when they had gone a long time without eating on the ship, Paul stood up, and spoke in a persuasive tone: "Gentlemen, we did not have a discussion group before we sailed; but it is not too late. I propose we go into huddles of 10 or 12 in different parts of the ship and consider the status quo, and possible alterations of it which will be feasible in the near future." So they went into huddles and continued the discussion until they reached land.

"We understand that your point of view is discredited everywhere," announced the leading laymen of the First Church of Rome. "You do not understand," gently responded the apostle; "This is nothing which a little group conversation and committee work will not clear up. A little give-and-take will enable each of us to appreciate the contributions of other groups and perhaps you may then be willing to tolerate my rather unusual point of view."

And Amos stopped in the market place and cried: "It is clear that the voice of history is declaring that this is the century of Samaria. Yet it would be futile to assume that there are not some slight discrepancies between our formal profession and our actual behavior at times. I would suggest that Amaziah

116

be our group leader, and that we share our knowledge and pool our ignorance that we may come out with some conclusion which can be reported to the public at the next panel forum."

A Pharisee went up on the temple and he prayed thus with himself: "Lord, I thank you that I am not like other men; I do not undertake to act without the justification of group-thinking; I do not even criticize myself as such disparagement can impair the contribution one can make toward a sharing of better attitudes."

And Nicodemus, named by *Death* magazine as one of the ten great preachers of the Jews, came by night, and questioned, "How can a man be born again?" And the answer came clearly, "Well, what do you think about it?"

AMOS, 1971

The words of Amos, who was among the hill farmers of Appalachia, which he spoke in the days of Ahaz, who was the ruin of his country.

"Thus speaks the Eternal, 'For three crimes of North Vietnam and for four, I will not sidetrack the punishment thereof,' for its people have tortured in the jungle and have wrought destruction in the villages. And I will drop flame upon the porticoes of Hanoi and it shall perish with tumult, and I will eliminate the dictator and liquidate the commissars,' says the Eternal.

"So speaks the Eternal, 'For three sins of China and for four, shall punishment be inescapable, for its leaders have broken down the homes of their people and have murdered millions. Therefore shall rain fire upon them to consume, and shall leave no remnant of the cruel chairman,' " says the Eternal.

"Again the Eternal announces, 'For three transgressions of Russia and for four, shall it not escape disaster. For its rulers have murdered millions in their madness and have enslaved them that were free and pity is not in their vocabulary. Therefore shall fire come down upon Moscow and the palaces of the Kremlin shall melt,' adds the Eternal.

"And again the Eternal is broadcasting, 'For three crimes of Germany and for four, shall its punishment be certain, because it plotted two wars of terror and burned millions of my people in ovens and plots a third conflagration. There shall be returned upon Germans what they have done unto others and their sons shall suffer for their cruelties,' declares the Eternal.

"The Eternal has not gone off the air. 'For three exploitations of France and for four, I will not diminish the sure penalties thereof, for its merchants oppressed the peasants of Cambodia and exploited the villagers of the Niger and made Paris a poison to the world. Therefore shall I bring Paris down to the dust and guillotines shall flourish again by the Seine,' adds the Eternal.

"The Eternal has other countries on His list, 'For three crimes of the Low Countries and for four, they shall never escape the consequences, for their greed cut off the hands of toilers of the Congo and butchered the backwoodsmen of Indonesia and poured forth insane malice on the natives of the Cape. Therefore shall their apartheid be a separation from Me, and their enemies round about shall demolish them, and their long trek shall be their last, for they shall be no more,' says the Eternal.

"And the Eternal is not through sounding His irresistible verdicts. 'For three transgressions of England and for four, I will not avert the inevitable consequences of exploitation. For they became rich on the hunger of the Hindus and the misery of the Midlands and in their arrogance owned the oceans. Therefore shall fire fall upon Windsor and destruction descend on the Tories of Downing Street,' insists the Eternal.

"And the Eternal has a doom for my own country of the South. 'As you have bombed little children and buried hoods from churches, explosions shall rock your churches and shatter your ranchhouse windows. Inasmuch as you have voted for the waters of hate, so shall the cruel hate of others come upon you. As you enslaved My people even so shall your sons be enslaved. Because you have substituted the machine for the hungry sharecropper whom you swindled at the commissary, therefore shall the machine mow you down and you

118

shall no longer grind the face of the poor and your white houses shall have an end,' swears the Eternal.

"And the Eternal has a word for these United States, for His verdicts are plain. 'For three transgressions and for four will I not save you from the flames of destruction. For you betrayed brothers into the slavery of the slums and you poisoned the poor for a penny and the baby for a dirty dime. You robbed the migrant of his last dollar and oppressed the working man and smashed his unions and enslaved the farmer. You worship the bitter Baal of greed and degrade your daughters to the Ashtaroth of disease and death and burn sons to the Moloch of militarism. And your rich white trash shall burn and your poor white trash shall be obliterated and white power shall be blanched and black power blackened with smoke, that you may know that power belongs to the Eternal,' He reminds you.

" 'I brought you out of the bondage of Britain and gave you a continent and a land of freedom. But your heart has been lifted up and you seek to steal the stars and to massacre on the moon and to set my planets in disorder. You have exhausted the reserve of millennia in a century and wasted the precious oil on your aimless chariot riding. You cut down the forests and ruined the rivers and stripmined the Cumberlands and left mountain men homeless and hungry.

" 'The land you stole from the Indian shall be taken from you and given to a strange people who shall herd you in the desert and diminish you with fraud and firewater and the land shall be red. Sadistic Shermans shall burn from one Northern sea to another. And oily billionaires shall perish in the jungle and the manufacturers of napalm shall be burned with it.'

"Hear the word of the Eternal, 'Because you force cancer on your mothers and delirium tremens on your daughters, Milwaukee shall sink under the foam of destruction and the distilleries of Louisville shall be dynamited and cancer shall consume Carolina and the deadly cars of Detroit shall demolish it. Because you have poisoned the sky and polluted the water, the heavens shall become brass to suffocate whoever remains. And Pittsburgh shall be a wilderness and fish shall swim over the tall towers that were Wall Street. And supermarkets

shall cease and mailorder houses evaporate and department
stores disappear and jewelry melt and bankers be bankrupted
and loansharks lynched. Nor will I make an end,' guarantees
the Eternal.

" 'Because criminals are your masters and gangsters rule
over you, the billions they have piled up shall be swept away
and they shall kill off each other in madness until none remain. Because you have scattered disease among my poor
and sabotaged Medicare and sold medicine at unconscionable
profit, the Lord shall send a famine of healing upon the land.
Since you have tried to void my ordinances by deception, the
children of others shall inherit your treasures. Because judges
have refused justice to the needy, they have doomed themselves
to destruction. Because you have been overfed and richly
clothed while millions hungered and shivered in the cold, your
suburbs shall be ashes,' declared the Eternal.

" 'Hear the Word of the Eternal, you bloated white trash in
splitlevel palaces who crush the needy, who poison the poor.
Woe unto your fat cows who urge you on in alcoholic arrogance; their painted faces shall wither and their lustreless tresses
become uglier and when the Eternal is finished, not even a
microscope will discover a trace of you. And you who have
counterfeited My death shall learn that I am alive when I
set free death on the freeways. And I will eradicate your
universities and bring low your high schools because they
have deceived my daughters and my sons with lies. Your
malicious magazines shall be ground to pulp and your newspapers without news shall evaporate and your sinister screens
be silent and there shall be a famine for facts and none shall
assuage it,' adds the Eternal.

"For the Eternal insists, 'The day of the Eternal shall be
utter dark upon you, with no light in it. Are you any better
to Me than Cambodians or Cherokees? Because you follow
cruel faces fabricating daily falsehoods, the White House shall
be blackened with smoke and justice shall be done to your
justices and torture recoil on who allowed it. The bacteria
you prepare for others shall slay you, your missiles shall ex-
plode on your shopping centers, your drinking water shall

become death. And the pride of the Pentagon shall become a roost for buzzards and lizards shall lounge over Canaveral and as you have flown over all peoples, so shall they rain bombs on your babies, and 90 Nagasakis and 100 Hiroshimas shall descend upon you. And Republicans shall be ambushed on the highways and racists on the interstates, until you learn that the judgments of the Eternal are true and righteous altogether,' repeats the Eternal.

" 'And bishops shall blaze in pain and district superintendents disappear because you persecuted My messengers who told you the truth. The day of the Lord shall come upon the cruel commissars of cathedrals and the smug executives of Manhattan and the high-priced evangelists who betray me to sinister sadists. Those you have hired to assure you that I will tolerate your transgressions and that you can buy your way into heaven shall perish for their blasphemy,' " declares the Eternal.

"A final word from the Eternal. 'Let no Bishop Amaziah fool you. The Eternal is not to be mocked. I hate your smug suburban services and your high celebrations of your own glory and your callous conferences and cruel conventions which you blaspheme by My name. I delight not in crooning choirs or in tinpanny pianos or in budgets and programs. Forget your mammoth monuments to Mammon and your graying cathedrals of greed and your smooth sermons to comfort cruel cowards and your cash sprinkled with holy water. No! If you want to worship the Eternal, you can only do so through justice running like an irresistible mighty river through church and capitol and courthouse and college and through righteousness as a flowing fountain through childhood and commerce and culture. Then, if you will return from the evil of your ways and turn unto the Eternal, I will give unto you to be secure in joy forever in a spring with many summers in its hearts,' assures the Eternal."

NEITHER COUNT I MY LIFE DEAR

But none of these things move me, neither count I my life dear unto myself, that I may finish my course with joy, and the ministry, which I have received of the Lord Jesus.

Acts 20:24

The apostle declares that he is going to Jerusalem, knowing that in every city imprisonment awaits him, but he counts his life of no value save as it so spent in the service of Jesus. Moses counted not his life dear to himself when striking down arrogant exploiters, defending the helpless, challenging a haughty pharaoh, leading an ungrateful multitude through the wilderness. Last year I was given a volume inscribed "To the troubler of Israel" and it was good to be counted in the company of Elijah who disturbed by witnessing against the proud priests of Baal. The shy, poetic, affectionate Jeremiah was hated by false priests as he spent his years as a messenger of the Eternal against the injustice of government and the insincerity of religion. Amos counted his life of no value as he exposed the arrogant patrioteers, bribed judiciary, dishonest business, alcoholic leaders and hollow religion of his day. Socrates was unsilenced by jealous hate when he told Athenians "I believe to this day that no greater good has come to this state than my service to God."

Martin Luther noted, "Love of my neighbor includes enduring trouble, labor, ingratitude and contempt in the church on behalf of everyone who is in need of help." John Wesley wrote often, "I preached yesterday at this church; I will not be asked to preach there again." Our civilization has grown in human rights because Paul went to heathen courts to expose a church which convicted him without giving him an opportunity to defend himself.

John the Baptist counted not his life dear unto himself when he rebuked a gangster who could kill him, and who did, saying, "It is not lawful." So Nathan challenged David: "Those art the man." As John Jay Chapman wrote, "The truly religious man is willing at any moment to cast in the whole of life and leave the outcome to God."

Laws break those who violate them. Sin is lawlessness, anarchy, doing what you please. Judgment is the declaration of what is, of the realities of existence. The commandments are reality: envy injures the envious, falsehood debases the liar, stealing devaluates all property, lust brutalizes, murder degrades the value of all life, lack of love for parents recoils on the loveless, a day of rest gives strength, all names deserve reverence, idolatry makes man less than man. Shipwreck came to the centurion and his ship because he listened to the owner of the ship rather than to Paul. Millions were hungry in the Hoover depression because the masters of money would not heed warnings. We have been immersed in war because we listened to the voice of profits rather than to the voice of prophets. To send missionaries would have been not only less expensive but also more practical.

Those who rebuke the lawless have been the constructive leaders of history. The more Puritanism, the more democracy, the more learning, the more science, the more trust in God. Care for the prisoner and the insane began with the Puritans. The Puritans saw it is no more lawful to murder your neighbor with a bottle than with a gun.

The burden of the Lord has been upon me all my years, as on all the prophets, as on all who take God seriously. The burden of the Lord hangs heavy over our lives as it did over their lives. Too many preach against sin in general but never specify. Who preaches against the idol of the automobile, the cult of football? I have had to say "It is not lawful," when that is the word of the Lord. How many sermons disturb mean old women or meaner old men? I have moved from a liberal to a moderate to a conservative without moving an inch, but I have never been accused of "the easy speeches that comfort cruel men."

The mark of a genuine messenger is that he has a message, and that he is free to give it. I have belled the cats. What other commentator has cried out for 36 years "It is not lawful"? I have challenged presidents, senators, governors, college presidents and lesser lights: "It is not lawful." I have stood up against bishops swindling, stealing, lying, forcing out honest men. Augustine wrote "He who loves to govern rather than to do good is no bishop" and Wesley noted "The will of the king does not bind unless it is written in the law, how much less that of a bishop."

When church members counted themselves unworthy of eternal life, Paul turned to the Gentiles, to the unchurched. As Jesus took the straight road to Jerusalem rather than the safe road back to Galilee, so the apostle took the way of the cross. Although he was a churchman who loved the church, he could not betray God by letting himself be imprisoned in ecclesiastical routine. God has other channels available. People can be reached where they are by radio, classroom, press, government. After years of this Pauline ministry to the Gentiles, it was encouraging to hear the World Council of Churches and the Anglican Congress urge the church go beyond its front door and exercise the ministry we have been fulfilling in the rolling years.

"The times went over him" records the chronicler of a king. Times go over all of us, the tragic '20s, the hopeful '30s, the fateful '40s, the fatuous '50s, the stupid '60s, the sinister and suffocating '70s. Yet decades need not make us give in to helplessness or hopelessness. Life is not what you make it, but it is what you let it be.

God needs men to carry on His work in our age. "Man wanted" was Jeremiah's advertisement, but he could not find one real man in the city of 300,000. Men are scarce in any place, in any organization. Life separates the men from the boys and does not make the boys generals. Men are people who are mature, responsible, free; they are marked by initiative, courage, willingness to wade in when the water gets deep, to stand up and be counted. The last pages of the Bible remind us that cowards never get to heaven. After 5 of the 85 present at a church council blocked the illegal greed of a bishop, most of the rest came up afterward to say they were behind us. They were—way behind. Men try to tell the truth. Men can take defeat and keep on fighting. Jesus needed men. On Good Friday, where were the 5,000? The 4,000? The 70? The 12?

God give us men! A time like this demands
Strong minds, great hearts, true faith and ready hands,
Men whom the lust of office does not kill,
Men whom the spoils of office can not buy,
Men who possess opinions and a will,
Men who have honor, men who will not lie.
Tall men, sun-crowned, who live above the world
In public duty and in private thinking. . . .
Wrong rules the world and waiting justice sleeps.

The men God wants are those who will receive His spirit, not of fear, but of love and of power and of a sound mind. God has not given us a spirit of fear. We are not afraid. The Lord is our Helper and we will not fear what man can do to us. A spirit of love sends us to help all we meet. He gives us power. Going to worship does not make you a better Christian unless you bring home power to help others. It does no good to go to the grocery and not bring home groceries. We learn to walk today and tomorrow and the day after. The Christian is the only sane person, he recognizes realities. He learns to walk in lowly paths of service free.

"Let thy mercy come to light, as the years roll their courses," prayed Habbakuk. You do not have to let the evil of the rolling years submerge you, nor the false alluring quicksands of sin drag you down. This is the Year of the Pig in China, and in some other places. Our 1970 stamp of the Age of the Reptiles was appropriate. You do not have to let others make up your mind or let sand be thrown in your eyes by those picking your pockets or surrender to rising hate. You do not have to give in to the tyranny of iron, bamboo, magnolia or flickering curtains. Milovan Djilas wrote from a Communist prison "The strongest are those who renounce their own times and become part of those yet to come." On his last day on earth the Irish martyr Roger Casement who had exposed Belgian atrocities in the Congo, observed, "I've done my work anyhow and some evils will never be the same."

After preaching this message at a church in the San Francisco area, I was told by a teacher that she had resigned her position in a slum school, but that after hearing the sermon she had decided to return to the school in the slums. I assured her I did not always get such fast results in Mississippi. But it was part of the inspiration by which I count not my life dear unto myself, that I may finish my course with joy, and the ministry, which I have received of the Lord Jesus.

Teach us, good Lord, to serve Thee as Thou deservest; to give and not to count the cost; to fight and not to heed the wounds; to toil and not to seek for rest; to labor and not to ask for any reward, save that of knowing we do Thy will, in Jesus Christ our Lord.

WHAT MEAN YOU BY THESE STONES?

Joshua 4:6

Stones gray and fading in the quiet country churchyard immortalized by Thomas Gray memorialize the short and simple annals. The present needs to be reminded of a more peaceful and more permanent past. This is why Joshua commanded stones of memory to be set up for the enlightenment of future generations.

Stones memorialize the heroes of peace, who faithfully did their work in store, office, factory and highway, who tilled the soil, kept the home, taught the children, navigated the government, wrote and preached the truth. Those who have passed this way before speak to us from these stones. Unless we keep faith with them, these stones mean little.

Stones in old cemeteries remind us of those who fought to proclaim liberty throughout all the land to all the inhabitants thereof. These stones mean exactly nothing unless we practice that all men are created equal, unless we give all their inalienable rights, unless we know all God's children have wings, unless we give liberty and justice to all. Until the poorest miner in the most backward county in Kentucky is free, we are not a land of liberty.

What do these stones say which mark those of a century ago who died for different definitions of freedom? They did not fight for hate. We betray them and their stones are meaningless if the America they loved disappears and the freedom they cherished vanishes. What do we mean by the stones of 1918 and 1944? Nothing, unless we stop following the same path of militarism at home and abroad which led to these wars. We did not remember Pearl Harbor and criminally negligent admirals and generals went unpunished and the treasonable paper which stole and published our military secrets for the enemy continues on its treasonable career. We have already betrayed these stones as we have made ready for a third war the evil power which began these two and as we arm dictators against their people.

What do we mean by these stones? Some mark those who died from poverty in a land of abundance, where the Judases see to it that by their stealing we have the poor always with us. Long lines of stones mark little children who died because their parents were too poor to pay for proper care. Stones mark the needy likewise. Every day we add 100 stones for those murdered by crime and vice, more for lives warped and ended by hate. Other stones mark those poisoned by lead in the mine, by radium in the factory, by food from the store. The toll of industry has been higher than that of warfare.

What mean you by these stones? Under them rest the bodies of miners killed in mines, when they were recovered. If Communists murdered 78 Americans in one day, we could be at war by sundown, but when 78 Americans are murdered by the careless greed of mineowners, we do exactly nothing.

The liberty for which their sons died never came to them. They owed their souls to the company store. Cheated, swindled, exploited, discarded, warped or murdered, their slavery has been more brutal than that of a century ago which had sense enough to care for its old, its young, its sick. Children of miners have known no freedom in schools furnishing little learning to keep down taxes on mineowners while colleges greedily grabbing for handouts from the company store train subservient peons and slick stoolpigeons to sell out their neighbors. The chief things of the everlasting mountains are boys and girls who could become men and women of character but instead their slavery is fortified by vice and alcohol by absentee colonial exploiters.

What mean you by these stones? Most miners who die in accidents are murdered by deliberate negligence of the mineowners. Every year 1 of 10 miners is injured, 1 of 100 killed. No one remembers when mineowners sent an armored train shooting into mine villages. Why is the law not enforced? The mine in which these 78 West Virginia miners were murdered by deliberate neglect had been caught the three preceding years with 7 dangerous practices and 31 pieces of dangerous equipment. Why not send to work in the mines the present administration which deliberately refuses to enforce the safety laws? Why not send those who closed their mines that miners have to work on their own with no standards of safety, wages, hours?

Their mine was sealed with 78 alive in it to die of slow suffocation. The air supply was choked to extinguish the fire. Why? To save the property of the mineowners. Is any mine worth the lives of 78 men? Not by American standards, not by the word of Jesus.

Why didn't they seal in the rich exploiters? Their lives would never be missed. Why didn't they seal in officials who refuse to enforce, governors who refuse to protest, senators who block safety? The contributions to the world of all of these are less than that of 78 working men. The curse of God is upon those responsible and they will be sealed in worse in eternity. "Mother" Jones said that when she got to heaven she was going to tell God about West Virginia. But West Virginia is in better shape than most mining states; it has even passed a law protecting the majority of the miners suffering from black lung. Why can't a nation dedicated to liberty and opportunity take care now of miners? What mean you by these stones? "We want to know," sobbed the wife of a trapped miner.

What mean you by these stones? A few stones remind us of a war of 70 years ago which we would rather forget and which rarely gets a line in our history textbooks. We fought with the Filipinos to free them from Spain and then turned

128

against them just as we did against the Vietnamese who supported us. The Philippine War is ugly reading for us.

Eighty American officers were courtmartialed for torturing, drowning and murdering Filipinos. General Jacob Smith ordered everyone on the island of Samar over 10 years old to be murdered and the 20th Kansas wiped out all the inhabitants of Calocan. When Theodore Roosevelt congratulated a general on murdering 600 men, women, and children, Mark Twain wrote:

> Not one word of what T. R. said came out of his heart. He knew perfectly well that to pen 600 helpless and weaponless people in a hole and massacre them in detail from a safe position on the heights above was no brilliant feat of arms—our uniformed assassins have dishonored the flag. Its white stripes should be painted black and its stars replaced by a skull and crossbones.

What mean you by these stones of Vietnam? They mark the longest and most useless war in our history. Why did our press and screen deliberately lie to us that we were winning when we were losing? German generals deliberately left reason behind in world wars. Most wars have been won in spite of generals; as Stewart Alsop reminds us, "almost all our generals have been wrong in all our wars." Most countries are dictated to by generals, but war is too important to be left to generals, and peace even more so. Why have we not been told that bombing wins no wars, that the air force never discovered 400,000 Chinese in Korea, that our opponents win in Vietnam without an air force? Psychopaths of the all or nothing species cherish the unwarranted illusion bombs will never fall on us. As G. K. Chesterton wrote early in this century:

> *The men that worked for England,*
> *They have their graves at home,*
> *And the bees and birds of England*
> *About the cross can roam.*

> *The men that died for England,*
> *Following a fallen star,*
> *Alas, alas for England*
> *They have their graves afar.*

But they that rule in England,
In stately conclave met,
Alas, alas for England,
They have no graves as yet.

What did we let politicians and militarists drag us into wasting $130 billion and more precious lives to keep in power little Hitlers who betrayed their people to the Japanese and the French? Why has it taken us years to learn that almost no one there or in the world, is on our side in this jungle murder, that these Hitlers may torture and terrorize while they sell arms to the Viet Cong? Why have we let the Pentagon sell us defense which can not defend and steal from the poor $1 trillion, plus $30 billion a year for this war? Why has Congress refused to tax the profiteers who are making billions out of this war? Why is it no secret that the safest place in Vietnam is by an oil truck, because oil companies pay the Viet Cong millions in American cash for protection? What else are we fighting for except to make a few billionaires richer? It is no secret that Communists favor our wasting our men and billions in Vietnam.

What mean you by these stones? The stones of Vietnam mark the road to Syracuse. The Athenian Empire of culture and glory was misled by lying Alcibiades into an insane military adventure of Syracuse and overextended in this useless war it went down to unending disaster, while Alcibiades sold out his people as a profiteering traitor. Athens had become powerful by defeating Persia which overextended itself at Marathon and Salamis. Rome began its tottering fall when it overextended itself into the black forests of the Rhine. Huns at Chalons, Arabs at Tours, went too far in their arrogance as did Charles of Sweden at Pultowa, French at Quebec, English at Saratoga. The snows of Russia were dipped with French blood as an empire went to pieces and the empire of Britain began its precipitous downfall on the bloody sands of Gallipoli. Hitler overextended at Stalingrad and was smashed. And our Alcibiades led us into irretrievable disaster, and we have come to our Syracuse. God have mercy upon us, for history will not!

William Vaughn Moody wrote prophetic words 70 years ago for a cruel and senseless Philippine War, words which no one seems to have noticed are even more appropriate today.

> Streets of the roaring town,
> Hush for him, hush, be still:
> He comes who was stricken down
> Doing the word of our will.
> Hush! Let him have his state,
> Give him his soldier's crown.
> The grists of trade can wait
> Their grinding at the mill,
> But he cannot wait for his honor,
>   now the trumpet has been blown;
> Wreathe love now for his granite brow,
>   lay love on his breast of stone.
>
> Toll! Let the great bells toll,
> Till the clashing air is dim.
> Did we wrong his parting soul?
> We will make it up to him.
> Toll! Let him never guess
> What work we sent him to.
> Laurel, laurel, yes;
> He did what we bade him do.
> Praise, and never a whispered word
>   but the fight he fought was good;
> Never a word that the blood on his
>   sword was his country's own heart's blood.
>
> A flag for the soldier's bier
> Who dies that his land may live;
> O banners, banners here
> That he doubt not nor misgive,
> That he heed not from the tomb
> The evil days draw near
> When the nation, robed in gloom,
> With its faithless past shall strive.
> Let him never dream that his bullet's
>   scream went wide of its island mark,
> Home to the heart of his darling land
>   where she stumbled and sinned in the dark.

I KNOW THE LORD HAS LAID HIS HANDS ON ME

The spiritual is right: I know the Lord has laid His hands on me. I knew it when I was nine years old walking home from church, that the Lord had called me to be another Moses. The Lord called me, as He calls everyone, though not always in the same way or to the same vocations. He called me through my saintly mother, through the preaching of my father, through the unfailing inspiration of my brother Augustus who went home early in my ministry, through the courage of my brother George, through the faith and hope and love of my wife Mary Elizabeth. The Lord laid His hands on me through hymns and sermons, books and churches, word and worship, friends and students, environment and circumstance, through Jesus Christ our Lord. As Jeremiah wrote,

> Then the Lord put forth His hand and touched me and the Lord said unto me, Behold, I have put my words in your mouth.

I know the Lord has laid His hands on me when I read the Word, when I preach it, when I pray, when I write, when I teach, when I work with the needy, when I labor in government, when I speak over radio to a congregation known only to God. I know it today as I begin my 41st year of preaching, with 22,593 sermons preached to the glory of God, Whose I am and Whom I serve.

I know the Lord has laid His hands on me because He opens new light from His Word, as I read it. I have read the New Testament through 1932 times since 1932. My mother wore out many a Bible and I am using her last Bible this morning. To learn the Bible at home from your father and mother is a sure way for God to guide you in youth. I believe the Bible is true. Why should anyone dare to preach who does not believe the great affirmations of the New Testament? My grandfathers and grandmothers, my father and mother attended great universities and smaller schools but learning did not lead

132

them to doubt because they had more than a little learning. Professors in college who were ignorant of much and students whom I had to help to pass their courses imagined they were too smart to believe the Word. I was sure that whatever these did not believe was probably true. As a trained historian, I am astounded at the unwillingness to accept history for which we have more evidence than for most other history. A historian does not postulate what a man must have said but tries to find out what he did say. The poetry of the Bible requires more imagination than restricted mentalities afford. Most are not curious enough to read it through once, and many can not afford to read it, as they would have to change their ways.

I am allegedly the most overeducated person in the South or in my church with 27 alma maters, 10 years of graduate work and 6 degrees, but I have too much education to believe I know more than the Word. Those whose reading is meager and inadequate are in no position to criticize it, but after reading 2 books a week for years, none of the 8,523 inspire as does this Book. The power of the Book in the present as its influence in the past is beyond that of any other. Lives are still being changed by contact with it. His Word is true from the beginning and it confirms that the Lord has laid His hands on me.

Many of my letters are signed "serenely" and mean it. With all my statistics, I may seem an unlikely student of the school of Port Royal, but I am much of a quietist. I do all I can up to a certain point and then leave the outcome to the Lord. Long ago I concluded that I do not control my life; events happen to me. I have never been sure whether I would stay where I was the year following but have left it up to the Lord to guide. The medieval Irish monks who threw away their oars so God alone would guide them are beyond me, but not far. With Frederick William Faber,

> *I do the little I can do*
> *And leave the rest to Thee.*

And with John Greenleaf Whittier,

133

I know not what the future hath
Of marvel and surprise. . . .
I only know I can not drift
Beyond His love and care.

Because of this implicit trust, I am a free man. I fear God too much to fear any man. It took me years to learn that the promise that "all things work together for good to them that love God" is plural, that it does not guarantee to any one but to the group who love God that His eternal purposes shall be fulfilled. As the pattern gives freedom to the sonnet writer, so I am free as I march daily to a different drum. I learned long ago to make a sacrifice hit and go out that another may score and win the game.

I am humbly grateful for all that the Lord has done through me, for bringing the Word to little churches and larger radio congregations, for opening doors and helping others to open them, for giving friends to strengthen and students to brighten our ministry, for letting me be the twig which turns the course of the mighty river of the years. I thought that some day I would reach a plateau of rest but the hills ahead are high.

"Does the road wind uphill all the day?"
"Yes, to the very end."
"Will the journey last the whole livelong day?"
"From morn to night, my friend."

I said that when I became 50, I was going to say all I wanted to, but my friends said they thought I had been doing that. When I became 60, I intended to write all the truth I know. I am sure much of it will not get beyond our paper curtain but the Lord has enabled me to send light into darkness and to expose much evil in state and school and church. For many years I have kept in my active file these words of Kierkegaard.

I have something definite on my conscience. There is something quite definite that I have to say and I have it so much on my conscience that I feel I dare not die without having uttered it. For the instant I die and leave this

134

world I shall be in the same instant infinitely far away in a different world where in the same second the question will be put to me "Hast thou uttered the definite message quite definitely?" And if I have not done so, what then?

I know the Lord has laid His hands on me because, like Moses, I have spent 40 years in the wilderness because the people I supposed would understand did not. Last summer in Aberdeen an old Negro man I do not know told me, "You laid the foundation." Some gains have been made for which we have fought over the long years but more remains to be done. If people had listened to the Word of the Lord preached over the long years, if they had heeded! But they would not heed and now they are reaping the crop of chaff and bitterweed we warned that they were sowing. The generation that refuses to cross the river still dies in the wilderness.

All the world knows that Mississippi is a wilderness, but so is every other state, every nation. The world is much like Mississippi. Mississippi is a wilderness, and Manhattan is a wilderness and Montgomery is a wilderness and Moscow, Milwaukee, Madrid, Munich and Manchester are wildernesses. Any place which fails to do the will of God predestines itself to remain a wilderness. I have preached as much as anyone on the problems of Mississippi but not all the racial crime is in Mississippi and Alabama, not all the hatred in the deep South. We can't sweep it all under the rug, as some others do. Those who exploit white in Appalachia, yellow in California and red in Carolina conceal their wilderness behind curtains of falsehood. One network shunted me from preaching on race relations and cooperating with the inevitable to a poetic sermon on trees which brought a record fan mail but did not disturb. Few outsiders have been willing to be more than summer soldiers and to share the long hard winters of our discontent.

I have known less race prejudice and more genuine understanding in our part of Mississippi than in most places I have been. Much of the racism in the state is stirred up by the Judases owned by outside interests who keep us the poorest of states. Mississippi is a colony and we are colonials whose lives are run by outside exploiters. When the head of the Northern

135

Presbyterian Church told us at the Montreal World Council of Churches that freedom riders were to be sent to Mississippi, I thanked him, assuring that all of us need missionaries. But I asked, "Are you going to bring us more industries? More money for our agriculture? Are you going to give him 40 acres and a mule in this Second Reconstruction or send him back again to old massa?"

I have been known for a lifetime as a major voice in Mississippi for liberty and justice to all and for 30 years as the only white minister in the state with an honorary degree from a black college in the state. But in the area in which I have served the most underprivileged person has been the poor white, for whom I have been concerned. There are more slaves in the cancer South than in the cotton South, though they are hidden behind textile and tobacco curtains, while few blacks in the deep South are more hopelessly underprivileged than thousands of whites in Appalachia.

A voice crying in the wilderness need not expect it to immediately begin to blossom like the rose but it is distressing to see the few flowers trampled on. The Lord has rewarded me with better places but the poor sheep I have had to leave behind have been helpless and hopeless with hogs. I know the Lord has laid His hands on me because He has given me the message He gives all prophets, to set a trumpet against the house of the Lord, to smite and smash the altar of injustice, to insist God will destroy His own holy temple if it does not care for the poor and needy. As Piers Plowman saw centuries ago

> My dwelling not in court or cloister
> But on the road from Jericho
> I come with a wounded man.

A voice in the wilderness is heard by few and the mass media exist to keep you from hearing the voice. You are not allowed to know what happens in war or peace, who murders presidents or poor folks, how a handful of billionaires determine our destinies and do not let the peons know it. I have never seen a truthful article on Mississippi, though I have seen some

136

consisting of accurate statements, which is not the same. My truthful American History was ignored because it would upset too many profitable applecarts. As a most accurate predictor of elections and other events and a most truthful newscaster, I have been kept in the wilderness. I have been telling it like it is for a lifetime and have survived to be the elder elder of my church in the state and the senior preacher of all denominations in my section of it.

Colleges are more dishonest than churches, but no congregation is hunting for a man to make it hear the deep and disturbing words of Galilee. The percentage of Christians in the ministry is high, but the deep uncompromising gospel is not heard from most pulpits. Narrow still is the way and few there be that find it. Go to the stores and find how many business men follow Jesus; go to the homes and find how many women follow Him. No community concerned for its children would tolerate the poison of screen and print to which youth is cunningly and cruelly exposed. Organized religion, like organized government, organized business, organized education is run by the heartless insolence of the cash register. Reading the New Testament will make you out of place in any ecclesiastical organization or in any other organization. No follower of Jesus can possibly feel at home in the business, education, recreation or government of today. If after preaching 40 years and living 60 a man is not free to speak the truth, he never will be in this world.

After sixty summers and sixty springs,
I know an eternal springtime sings.

More and more our lives become like Henry Van Dyke's tremendous story of "The Other Wise Man." We have spent the jewels of life to help some suffering child of God. If you spend your life for those who are in need, you will find Jesus. There is no other way to walk in lowly paths of service free, until we come to the shining way. I know the Lord has laid His hands on me.

Do You?